Brilliant Laptops

Sandra Vogel

Prentice Hall
is an imprint of

Harlow, England • London • New York • Boston • San Francisco • Toronto • Sydney • Singapore • Hong Kong
Tokyo • Seoul • Taipei • New Delhi • Cape Town • Madrid • Mexico City • Amsterdam • Munich • Paris • Milan

Pearson Education Limited
Edinburgh Gate
Harlow CM20 2JE
United Kingdom
Tel: +44 (0)1279 623623
Fax: +44 (0)1279 431059
Website: www.pearsoned.co.uk

First edition published in Great Britain in 2010

© Pearson Education Limited 2010

The right of Sandra Vogel to be identified as author of this work has been asserted
by her in accordance with the Copyright, Designs and Patents Act 1988.

Pearson Education is not responsible for the content of third party internet sites.

ISBN: 978-0273-71575-7

British Library Cataloging-in-Publication Data
A catalogue record for this book can be obtained from the British Library

Library of Congress Cataloging-in-Publication Data
A catalog record for this book is available from the Library of Congress

Microsoft product screen shots reprinted with permission from Microsoft Corporation.

10 9 8 7 6 5 4 3 2 1
14 13 12 11 10

Typeset in 11pt Arial Condensed by 30
Printed and bound by Rotolito Lombarda, Italy

The publisher's policy is to use paper manufactured from sustainable forests.

Brilliant guides

What you need to know and how to do it

When you're working on your computer and come up against a problem that you're unsure how to solve, or want to accomplish something in an application that you aren't sure how to do, where do you look? Manuals and traditional training guides are usually too big and unwieldy and are intended to be used as end-to-end training resources, making it hard to get to the info you need right away without having to wade through pages of background information that you just don't need at that moment – and helplines are rarely that helpful!

Brilliant guides have been developed to allow you to find the info you need easily and without fuss and guide you through the task using a highly visual, step-by-step approach – providing exactly what you need to know when you need it!

Brilliant guides provide the quick, easy-to-access information that you need, using a table of contents and troubleshooting guide to help you find exactly what you need to know, and then presenting each task in a visual manner. Numbered steps guide you through each task or problem, using numerous screenshots to illustrate each step. Added features include 'For your information' and 'Timesaver tip' boxes that give you useful tips and information, while 'Did you know?...' sections alert you to relevant expert tips, tricks and advice to further expand your skills and knowledge. And 'Jargon buster' panels help you understand the terminology.

In addition to covering all major office PC applications, and related computing subjects, the *Brilliant* series contains titles that will help you in every aspect of your working life, such as writing the perfect CV, answering the toughest interview questions and moving on in your career.

Brilliant guides are the light at the end of the tunnel when you are faced with any minor or major task.

Publisher's acknowledgements

We are grateful to the following for permission to reproduce copyright material:

Screenshots on page 73, page 79, page 82, page 99, page 100, page 101, page 102, page 129, page 130, page 139, page 150, page 151, page 194, page 195, page 196, page 198, page 199, page 201, page 217, page 220, page 236, page 241 from Microsoft, Microsoft product screenshots reprinted with permission from Microsoft Corporation; Screenshot on page 78 from http://totalhotspots.com, Total Hotspots Ltd; Screenshot on page 117 from AVG Anti-Virus Free Edition, AVG Technologies; Screenshot on page 118 from http://www.zonealarm.com/store/content/company/aboutUs/pressroom/graphicResourcesZA.jsp?dc=12bms&ctry=US&lang=en, 2009 © Check Point Software Technologies Ltd; Screenshot on page 122 from Facebook Sign Up page, http://www.facebook.com/, used under licence with the permission of Facebook; Screenshot on page 122 from www.ask.com, © IAC Search & media, Inc. 2009. All rights reserved. ASK.COM, ASK JEEVES, the ASK logo, the ASK JEEVES logo and other trade marks appearing on the Ask.com and Ask Jeeves websites are property of IAC Search & Media, Inc. and/or its licensors; Screenshot on page 128 from OpenOffice.org.Writer, http://www.openoffice.org/product/pix/writer-big.bmp, screenshots used by permission of the OpenOffice.org Marketing Project, http://marketing.openoffice.org; Screenshot on page 128 from OpenOffice.org Calc, http://www.openoffice.org/product/pix/calc-big.bmp, screenshots used by permission of the OpenOffice.org Marketing Project http://marketing.openoffice.org; Screenshot on page 128 from www.zoho.com, Zoho; Screenshot on page 136 from http://www.mozilla.com/en-US/press/image-library/screenshot-thunderbird-message.png, copyright 2005-2009 Mozilla. All Rights Reserved. All rights in the names, trademarks, and logos of the Mozilla Foundation, including without limitation, Mozilla®, Thunderbird®, as well as the Thunderbird logo are owned exclusively by the Mozilla Foundation. All other trademarks, service marks and trade names appearing in this document are the property of their respective owners; Screenshots on page 139, page 140, page 140, page 146 from Microsoft screenshot frame reprinted with permission from Microsoft Corporation; Screenshot on page 142 from http://www.realnetworks.com/company/press/resources.html, Copyright © 1995-2008 RealNetworks, Inc. All rights reserved. RealPlayer is the registered trademark of RealNetworks, Inc; Screenshot on page 149 from http://www.2brightsparks.com/syncback/syncback-hub.html, 2BrightSparks Pte Ltd; Screenshot on page 178 from Add Contact 4 screen shot, http://www.flickr.com/photos/skypeconversations/sets/72157607505702184/, Skype Limited; Screenshot on page 222 from http://www.zonealarm.com/security/en-us/zonealarm-pc-security-free-firewall.htm, 2009 © Check Point Software Technologies Ltd; Screenshot on page 223 from AVG Anti-Virus

Free Edition, Scan whole computer, AVG Technologies; Screenshot on page 223 from Norton 360 Version 4.0 All-in-One security, with permission from Symantec; Screenshot on page 224 from http://www.zonealarm.com, 2009 © Check Point Software Technologies Ltd.

In some instances we have been unable to trace the owners of copyright material, and we would appreciate any information that would enable us to do so.

Author's acknowledgements

The author would like to thank Michael Browne, Tony Burton and Jackie Olive for reading the text and providing useful comments and advice. She would also like to thank Steve and Katy at Pearson for their patience and hand-holding.

About the author

Sandra Vogel has been a computer enthusiast since learning to program her first computer – a Sinclair Spectrum. She has been writing about computers full time for more than 10 years and has written several books, written articles for national newspapers and worked for many of the UK's leading computer magazines and websites.

Contents

Introduction

Welcome to *Brilliant Laptops*, a visual quick-reference book that shows you how to make the most of your laptop computer, particularly if it is your first one, or if you are new to the world of computers! It will give you a solid grounding on how to choose the right laptop for you, how it works and how to get the best out of your laptop – a complete reference for the beginner and intermediate user who hasn't grown up with a laptop.

Find what you need to know – when you need it

You don't have to read this book in any particular order. We've designed the book so that you can jump in, get the information you need, and jump out. To find the information that you need, just look up the task in the table of contents or Troubleshooting guide, and turn to the page listed. Read the task introduction, follow the step-by-step instructions along with the illustration, and you're done.

How this book works

Each task is presented with step-by-step instructions in one column and screen illustrations in the other. This arrangement lets you focus on a single task without having to turn the pages too often.

Step-by-step instructions

This book provides concise step-by-step instructions that show you how to accomplish a task. Each set of instructions includes illustrations that directly correspond to the easy-to-read steps. Eye-catching text features provide additional helpful information in bite-sized chunks to help you work more efficiently or to teach you more in-depth information. The 'For your information' feature provides tips and techniques to help you work smarter, while the 'See also' cross-references lead you to other parts of the book containing related information about the task. Essential information is highlighted in 'Important' boxes that will ensure you don't miss any vital suggestions and advice.

Troubleshooting guide

This book offers quick and easy ways to diagnose and solve common problems that you might encounter, using the Troubleshooting guide. The problems are grouped into categories.

Spelling

We have used UK spelling conventions throughout this book. You may therefore notice some inconsistencies between the text and the software on your computer which is likely to have been developed in the USA. We have however adopted US spelling for the words 'disk' and 'program' as these are commonly accepted throughout the world.

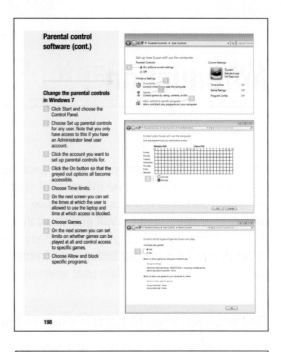

Why buy a laptop?

Introduction

This book is designed to help you choose a laptop computer and then to get the most from it.

It is suitable for you if you are:

- considering buying your first computer.
- upgrading from an older computer to a newer one, either a desktop or a laptop.
- learning to use your new laptop computer.

This is not the kind of book that you have to read from cover to cover. You could choose to take that approach, and we have organised the chapters so that they take you through things in a logical sequence. Alternatively you could dip into the chapters that seem most suitable to read at any one time.

Whichever method you choose this book should help you with the following:

- getting the information you need to make a decision to purchase the right laptop for you.
- making choices about the extras you might need such as software and hardware add-ons.
- understanding your new laptop's key features.
- using your computer in a safe and secure way.
- making the best use of your laptop.

What you'll do

Why buy a computer?

Why choose a laptop?

Are laptops a compromise?

Where laptops have the edge

What else do you need?

We start in this chapter by covering the very first steps:

- answering the question 'why buy a computer?'
- answering the question 'why make it a laptop?'
- thinking about budgeting for the overall cost.

Timesaver tip

If you come across words or ideas that you don't understand, then flip over to the **Jargon buster** at the back of the book. This provides definitions of the computer jargon used in this book.

People buy computers for all kinds of reasons: it all depends on what you want to do with the computer.

Some uses for computers include:

■ household management (e.g. keeping track of finances, writing important letters, tracking home management projects).

■ family activities (e.g. allowing children to do schoolwork, to keep in touch with their friends by email or to use the Internet for school research).

■ large projects such as family history research.

■ writing a novel.

■ organising your music – you can copy music from a computer onto portable music players.

■ helping to run a local club or society.

■ keeping in touch with family and friends by email or via the Internet, for example making video calls to relatives who live abroad.

Important

If you have not yet bought a computer think carefully about what you would like to use it for before making your purchase. Some laptops are more suitable than others for certain tasks.

Did you know?

Laptops come in lots of sizes with many different designs. Many have black, silver or white casings, but some have a more unique colour scheme.

Why choose a laptop?

Increasingly people decide to buy laptop computers rather than desktop versions. There are many reasons for making this choice.

It is obvious that laptop computers are a smaller option than desktop computers, and this means they are easy to carry around not only within your home but to other places too.

Having a portable computer means you can use it in places that are convenient for you. If you have a quiet space at home, perhaps one which doubles as an office, then you can use it here when you need to concentrate on things. You can also move it into a family space if, for example, you want to show photographs stored on it to family or friends.

A portable computer can also be taken outside the home, so if you are going on holiday or a work trip you could take it with you.

Laptops are space saving and because they are small are easy to store away when not in use. This helps reduce clutter around the home, and can keep your laptop safe from being knocked or otherwise damaged.

Timesaver tip

Think about how often and how far you may want to transport your laptop. It may be a factor in deciding what type of laptop to buy (see Chapter 3).

Jargon buster

Laptop, notebook, portable: these terms are interchangeable and you will see all three used to describe laptops. We are sticking with **laptop** in this book, but if you see the other terms elsewhere, the information may be entirely relevant to you.

Only a few years ago laptops were generally much less capable than desktop computers, especially when you compared the features on offer with the price paid for them. The gap has narrowed considerably in recent years, and today it is possible to buy a laptop that can offer the same features as a desktop without compromising on price.

Of course, there are still vast differences in features and capabilities from one laptop to the next, and with some laptops costing four or more times the price of others you need to make your choice carefully. At the least expensive end of the market are laptops known as 'netbooks'. These are a relatively new phenomenon, the first ones having appeared late in 2007. The least expensive of these are relatively limited in features, but they do provide some basic computing capability at a low cost.

There are still some cases when a desktop computer may be a more appropriate choice for you. For example if you are a games fan you may be drawn to a laptop built for this purpose with a large screen and sophisticated graphics management, but such a laptop may not be very portable.

Similarly, if you are the kind of person who is likely to want to upgrade and add to your computer over time, you may find a desktop computer a better bet because laptops have far fewer upgrade options (see Chapter 5).

However, laptops are evolving all the time, and today's limitations may be overcome tomorrow. Furthermore, advances in laptop development in recent years mean that in many cases a laptop may well be perfectly suited to your needs. And there are many instances in which laptops have some significant advantages over desktop computers.

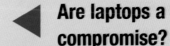

Are laptops a compromise?

1

Where laptops have the edge

There are several areas in which laptops have some strong plus points when compared to desktops. For example:

■ You can carry them with you. Depending on the size and weight of the laptop you choose it may be more or less convenient to carry around, but the portability could be very useful. This is the case both in the home and outside it. If you have one laptop in your home and it is to be shared by several people, or even if you like to do your computing in different places around your home at different times, a laptop is an ideal choice.

■ They take up less space. In the home you can put a laptop and its associated cables away in a drawer when not in use. Desktops tend to have large cases housing all their components, and as such they are difficult to keep out of view.

■ They can be used in many different locations. You could, for example, use your laptop on the train, take it on holiday with you, or even take it to a location like a library if you need to access some information there. Clearly this isn't possible with a desktop.

Did you know?

A key benefit of a laptop, when compared to a desktop computer, is that you can move it around easily from place to place, working in whatever location suits you best at the time.

Before you buy a laptop it is important to work out a budget. In addition to the laptop itself you may want to buy a range of other things, including software, hardware and some other extras.

A good starting point would be to make a list of all the possible things you could want to add to your laptop, both software and hardware. You may not be aware of all the possibilities at this stage, but you can add to the list as you read this book, or as you come across new ideas.

Some software may come with your laptop, which can help reduce the overall cost, but you won't know what comes with particular laptops until you start looking at what is available, so it's best to include everything you think you'll need in your list to start with.

You may decide you don't need to buy all the extras at the outset, and you shouldn't buy equipment unless you are sure you need it – you could use the money for something else instead!

Nevertheless having a list will both help you budget and help you think about the possibilities for your laptop.

Below is a list to get you started. We will cover these topics in more detail later on.

Hardware

- External keyboard.
- External mouse.
- External monitor.
- Printer.
- Scanner.
- Webcam for video calling over the Internet and other projects.
- External hard drive (for backups).
- Cardreader (for flash memory cards).
- USB keydrive for transferring information between computers.
- External speakers.

What else do you need? (cont.)

Timesaver tip

When it comes to software, you may find that free or low cost software is good enough to meet your needs (see Chapter 6).

Software

- Anti-virus software, anti-spyware, anti-malware.
- Word processing and spreadsheets.
- Music and video management.
- Family history management.
- Photo and video editing software.

Extras

- Carrying case.
- Laptop stand.
- Docking station or port replicator.
- Internet connection (regular monthly expense).
- Networking equipment (if you have more than one computer).
- Insurance.

What kind of user are you?

Introduction

Before you start to look at the various laptops currently available and make a buying decision, it is a good idea to think about the different kinds of ways you are likely to want to use your new laptop.

Naturally, you can't know every possible use right at the outset. One of the joys of having a laptop is that new possibilities open up to you only after you've got it. Also, as time goes by you will find that new interests and activities are suited to being managed on your computer and you can't possibly second-guess what these are likely to be. For example, you may not be terribly interested in family history at the moment, but if you become so in future your laptop could make the task of organising material and sharing it with family members much easier than simply using scraps of paper and a paper filing system.

It is also worth recognising what kind of purchaser you are. Do you rush out and buy things as soon as they are released onto the market, do you wait for the sales, are you an avid reader of consumer reports, and so on?

Knowing yourself in both these respects can help you to make well informed choices when it comes to purchasing, and to avoid some pitfalls. This should ensure you buy a laptop worthy of your requirements and one which will have a long and useful life.

What you'll do

Decide what type of user you are

Types of purchaser

Types of laptop user

Checklist of laptop uses and characteristics

Money matters

How much do you need to spend?

Warranties and insurance

Choosing a brand

Try before you buy

Decide what type of user you are

1. Decide how far and how often you are likely to want to carry your laptop.

2. Think about the different kinds of tasks you might use your laptop for. You can use the checklist later on in this chapter to help you.

3. Think about the various types of laptop and which one suits you best. You'll find some help on this in Chapter 3.

4. Work out the types of features you want. Again you'll find some help on this in Chapter 3.

Buyers and users

What follows are some types of buyer, and a set of fictional users with an illustration of the type of laptop that might suit them. Both should help you firm up your own ideas about your particular needs and point out some things to look out for along the way.

It is important to recognise that what follows is not meant to be a set of mutually exclusive options. That is to say, we don't expect that everybody will fall into one group and one group alone. You are much more likely to see characteristics that apply to you in more than one group.

This is perfectly fine – we are just trying to help you work out how you go about making a purchase and what you might use your laptop for. Laptops are so versatile that we couldn't possibly come up with a set of descriptions which would provide a perfect fit for every eventuality.

At the end of this chapter you will find a checklist. This is designed to help you come up with a set of laptop characteristics that will suit you best and should help you narrow down your choice of laptop.

The impulse buyer

You don't do a lot of research before going into a store to see what they have for sale. You look at the range on offer, possibly check out one or more competing shops, and make a purchasing decision quickly.

Our advice

This approach can result in some real bargains being purchased. You may come across 'end-of-line' laptops that a store wants to remove from stock before bringing in new models, for example, and these could be available relatively cheaply.

But equally you could find yourself falling victim to sales patter which talks up lesser models. If you have not done some research, telling the difference between the two could be difficult.

The sales fan

You prefer to buy goods in sales. You know you are likely to get end-of-line products this way, but feel that you get good value for money and don't need all the latest features.

Our advice

If you have done your research and know about the better brands, and the kinds of characteristics you are looking for in a laptop, and you are certain that you can live with models that are not at the leading edge, then this could be a good strategy.

Because laptop lines are 'refreshed' fairly regularly with new models you may well find that you do indeed get a bargain with this approach.

The economist

You like to get good value for money. You tend to shop around, read consumer reports, ask friends and family for advice, and make a buying decision after weighing up all the competing models and their pros and cons.

You take a while to make a final decision, because you expect your final purchase to be the best possible fit between price and performance, and you expect it to be a long time before you have to buy a replacement. You always check out the warranty arrangements when assessing competing models.

Our advice

There is nothing wrong with this approach which is a solid one when buying things like washing machines, vacuum cleaners and cars. It can also be applied to laptops, but needs to be done alongside considerations of what you will use your laptop for. There are better and less good buys for all the different types of user (see below) so choosing purely on the basis of value for money might not get you the best laptop for your needs.

You also need to bear in mind that the 'product cycle' for laptops is relatively short. New models are announced with what might appear to be bewildering frequency, in order that the latest components can be utilised in top of the range machines. For some popular brands the 'product cycle' can be as short as three months.

This means not only that prices can change very frequently (usually falling, which has to be a good thing from a buyer's point of view), but that if you take too long evaluating different models, the one you finally settle on may in fact have disappeared from a line-up.

The market leader

You are the kind of person who looks at what is available and chooses what you consider to be the most advanced, 'top of the range' model available at the time. Inevitably you pay a premium for choosing the very latest thing, but you consider this to be worth it in order to be at the cutting edge.

Unfortunately, in laptop terms you may also be buying features you don't actually want or need and can get caught up in a race you can't ever win. Laptop ranges are 'refreshed' with new models at frequent intervals and today's cutting edge machine won't be in that position in six months' time, or even in three months' time.

You may also face something of a dilemma in deciding what actually *is* the most advanced top of the range laptop. In the next chapter you will see a section on different types of laptop. As you read this you may come to the conclusion that 'top of the range' for one type is not the same as top of the range in another.

Our advice

Buying the latest thing puts you at the cutting edge for a short period of time. However, soon a new leading model will appear, and what you have will no longer be at the front of the range. If you have the money to spend on the very latest equipment, it might actually be better spent on the characteristics and components that best fit your needs.

Types of laptop user

The mobile user

- **What you want**. A laptop you can carry around from one place to the next easily.

- **Why you want it**. Perhaps you want to use your laptop both at home and at work, or you want to be able to take it with you on holidays or other trips away from home.

- **What to look for**. A small and light laptop. Good battery life is important as you'll be using your laptop away from mains power for a fair amount of time. Light weight will matter too. You may soon get tired of carrying a heavy laptop from one place to the next.

Points to consider:

- Take care that the screen and keyboard are both large enough for your needs. Some ultraportable laptops and netbooks have very small screens and keyboards. This helps to keep the overall weight down, but on the smallest of them the screen and keyboard might be impractical for some users.

- If you are considering a netbook because it is small make sure you are fully aware of its limitations. Is its storage space going to be enough for you? Is the screen going to be big enough? Is the keyboard too small for you to use comfortably?

- Ensure that there is an internal optical drive if you think you are going to need this. Not every ultraportable laptop or netbook has one.

- Consider future needs. You might not want a very large hard drive at the outset, but if you become interested in multimedia such as photography, music or movies you may need a lot of storage space. Upgrading a laptop hard drive is possible but may be daunting for the novice and could be more expensive than buying a larger hard drive at the outset.

Jargon buster

Optical drive: a reader and writer for optical media, typically CD or DVD. Optical drives can be used for a wide range of tasks including playing music CDs, playing commercially available DVDs such as movies, recording onto CD and DVD to make your own music CDs or video DVDs, or to store any files you want to keep.

Docking station: an add-on for your laptop that gives it a wider range of ports and connectors than are built into it. These can be useful if you want to connect lots of hardware when your laptop is on your desk.

The games player

- **What you want**. A laptop on which you can play the very latest computer games as well as performing a range of other tasks.

- **Why you want it**. You are a gaming fan, but do not want to have a large computer in your home and/or want portability.

- **What to look for**. You will need lots of RAM memory, a fast processor and a large hard drive as well as a big, high-resolution screen. A dedicated graphics chip is also important for games players. Compromising on any of these could cause problems.

You probably also want good sound output and may consider buying external speakers and/or headphones for the best sound experience you can get.

? Did you know?
Some laptops can be augmented with a docking station which adds more ports and connectors.

? Did you know?
You can buy external speakers to enhance the sound output from a laptop.

Types of laptop user (cont.)

Points to consider:

- Even the largest of laptop screens is not as large as an external monitor could be. If you are considering buying an external monitor, check the highest resolution your likely laptop can send to it.

- Graphics performance is key for you, but what is a state of the art specification today may not be so tomorrow. It is impossible to upgrade the graphics card in a laptop, much easier in a desktop.

- Laptops can be large and heavy, weighing in at around or over 5kg. This means it may not be very portable.

- You may want to buy an external mouse and keyboard to assist with gaming.

Jargon buster

Hard drive: the storage area of your computer. The hard drive is where all the documents and other materials you produce are stored, where all the applications you install are stored, and where the operating system is located.

The home user

- **What you want**. A laptop you can use primarily within your home. You may carry it to other places, but this is less important to you, and so you don't feel too concerned about buying a laptop that is very small and light.

- **Why you want it**. Primarily you are keen on household management type tasks such as writing and storing important letters, budgeting, and banking on the Internet. You want to keep in touch with friends and family by email. You also think you might buy a digital camera at some point and become more interested in photography as a hobby.

- **What to look for**. Most of your requirements are not very hungry as far as hard drive space is concerned, and you should be fine with a mid-range or lower laptop.

Points to consider:

- Consider your future hard drive space requirements and buy large enough to accommodate future digital photography storage. If space does become a problem you can store photos on DVDs or CDs, but this is a less satisfactory solution as you'll need to carry the disks around with you in order to share photos with other people.

- Look at different screen sizes in shops and try Web browsing and watching a DVD with them, if at all possible. You may find some screen sizes are more comfortable to use than others and widescreen formats are good for watching movies from DVD.

Types of laptop user (cont.)

The family

■ **What you want**. A single laptop for the whole family to share. You would like to keep it in one location in the home – probably the living room, so that you can watch what the children are doing – but you do not rule out moving it around the home and taking it when travelling.

■ **Why you want it**. You expect the children will want to use the laptop for the Web and for homework and email, while adults will want to write letters and do budget management as well as use the Internet and email.

■ **What to look for**. We suggest you look for a laptop that is solidly built and robust as it may get a little rough treatment because it is shared among so many users.

Points to consider:

■ Having many users on a single laptop can be a recipe for disaster if they all want to install their own software and set up the laptop to look and behave in a way that suits them best. Research setting up separate 'user accounts' for family members (see Chapter 8).

■ If there are going to be younger users consider parental control software. This lets you control what some users are able to do on a computer (see Chapter 8).

The student

- **What you want**. A capable but portable laptop that can handle the requirements of your course but also give you a little fun time too. Your budget is not limitless. You want to buy just one computer to last the duration of your course.

- **Why you want it**. A computer is essential for coursework and increasingly an important part of modern life in general.

- **What to look for**. Good value for money and a strong range of features including a large hard disk and a processor that can handle video playback. Portability is important too.

Points to consider:

- Ultraportable laptops are light and easy to carry, but can be expensive in comparison to their slightly larger slim and light cousins.

- Don't get drawn into buying an expensive gaming machine if you don't really need the large screen and expensive graphics features these often offer.

Checklist of laptop uses and characteristics

Use the table to make a note of the various activities you want to do with your laptop, and mark up how important they are. We suggest one or more characteristics to look for in a laptop that will help you with each activity. Then you can use the completed table to help you choose a laptop that best fits your needs.

You might like to photocopy the table before you start to fill it in. Then you can keep it by your side as you read the rest of this book and make notes to keep it up to date as you think more about your new laptop.

There is space in the table for you to add your own activities and if we have not provided enough room for this, just add more rows to the table to meet your requirements.

Activity	How important is it?	Things to look for in a laptop
Basic letter writing	☐ Very important ☐ Quite important ☐ Might be useful ☐ Not important at all	Good quality keyboard that you find easy to use. Bundled software that may include a word processing package.
General household budgeting	☐ Very important ☐ Quite important ☐ Might be useful ☐ Not important at all	Wide screen format. This should help make it easier to see more complicated spreadsheets.
Project planning (e.g. decorating or home/garden renovation)	☐ Very important ☐ Quite important ☐ Might be useful ☐ Not important at all	Wide screen format. This should help make it easier to see more complicated spreadsheets. Good quality keyboard that you find easy to use.
Email	☐ Very important ☐ Quite important ☐ Might be useful ☐ Not important at all	All laptops can manage email so there are no specific characteristics you should search for.
Web	☐ Very important ☐ Quite important ☐ Might be useful ☐ Not important at all	Some laptops have a built-in camera for video conferencing over the Internet. Wide screen format which can make it easier to see some websites in full.
Projects and hobbies such as family history, digital photography, storing music in digital format, managing information on collections, writing a novel, helping to run a local club or society	☐ Very important ☐ Quite important ☐ Might be useful ☐ Not important at all	Some hobby activities can result in the need to store lots of data: digital photography or having lots of music stored digitally, for example. Consider a larger hard drive if this is the case for you.

Activity	How important is it?	Things to look for in a laptop
Playing games	☐ Very important ☐ Quite important ☐ Might be useful ☐ Not important at all	A fast processor, large screen and good graphics capability will be important. Some laptops are designed specifically with games players in mind. A large hard drive may be required to store games on.
Children's schoolwork and leisure activities	☐ Very important ☐ Quite important ☐ Might be useful ☐ Not important at all	An external keyboard and mouse will help protect those built into your laptop from rough treatment and damage.
Watching movies on DVD	☐ Very important ☐ Quite important ☐ Might be useful ☐ Not important at all	A fast processor is recommended to help with data processing, and a wide screen will allow you to view movies in wide format. An internal optical drive is important, and it needs to be able to play DVDs. The laptop also needs to have good sound output which could be a combination of: good built in speakers; an accessible headphones jack; high quality output to external speakers; a large enough screen to let you view your work in progress clearly.
Designing poster, leaflets, etc. for clubs or work	☐ Very important ☐ Quite important ☐ Might be useful ☐ Not important at all	_____ _____ _____ _____
	☐ Very important ☐ Quite important ☐ Might be useful ☐ Not important at all	_____ _____ _____ _____
	☐ Very important ☐ Quite important ☐ Might be useful ☐ Not important at all	_____ _____ _____ _____
	☐ Very important ☐ Quite important ☐ Might be useful ☐ Not important at all	_____ _____ _____ _____

Money matters

Should you set a budget before you start to look at laptops, or check out the lie of the land first and then see what you can afford? Either is an acceptable place to start, but do be aware of the following important points:

- when you start looking around at laptops you may not have realistic expectations of what you can get for your money.
- you should be aware that 'impulse buys' at the time you purchase your laptop can add considerably to the overall purchase price.

On the first point, we are not suggesting that anyone thinks they can buy a laptop for almost nothing at all. But there are some incredibly low-priced laptops available at the moment, and inevitably some of the specifications are compromised to meet the low price.

This may not matter if all you need is a computer for some general word processing, Internet and household budget management. But as you start to think about more complex or space hungry tasks, you may find that the hard drives, processing power and even graphics capabilities of the very least expensive of laptops are not up to your requirements.

On the second point, impulse buys at the point of purchase can add considerably to your overall cost almost without you noticing it. For example, beware of being encouraged to buy additional software if you are not aware of the alternatives. There are, as we shall see later in this book, many excellent free and low-cost alternatives to popular and well known applications, and these, along with what comes as part of your laptop in the first place, really should be enough to make you productive in the early days at least. Many people find they can get along very well indeed without buying expensive software.

The same goes for 'peripherals' such as mice or keyboards. Many laptop owners find an external mouse and keyboard very useful when they are sitting at their own desk at home. But some are much more expensive than others, keyboards have many different key layouts and extra keys, and mice function in different ways.

It is a good idea to shop around and try before you buy when considering purchases like these.

When you start to think of a budget for your new laptop there are some general rules of thumb which dictate the kinds of computer and specifications you will get within a given price range.

Under £250

If you intend to spend less than £250 your options will be limited and you will not have access to many up to the minute features. However, you can buy a laptop for less than £250. You may particularly be drawn to one of the new breed of ultra low-cost laptops which we have mentioned before. Many people refer to these as netbooks. Most laptop manufacturers have a netbook in their range.

£251 to £450

You can get a very solid and dependable laptop within this price range. You aren't spending enough to get state of the art components, and you may find that a fair few compromises have been made to meet the price point. Perhaps the hard drive is small, the processor is mid-range, and the general build is adequate rather than outstanding. But if your needs run to a little letter writing and some email, this budget could suit you.

£451 to £899

You should be able to find a good range of laptops in this price bracket of all sizes and to suit most requirements. The components will be at the mid- to high-end with fast processors and large hard drives, high-quality screens, good battery life and robust build quality.

How much do you need to spend? (cont.)

Over £900

If you have more than £900 to spend on a laptop then you can start to look at state of the art computing marrying the latest components with sleek hardware designs. Our word of advice here is to ensure your money is spent on functions and not simply on brand name or good looks – unless, of course, that is what you like spending your money on!

It is very important to consider laptop insurance and warranties.

Warranties

When you buy your laptop it may come with a warranty. Check the terms of the warranty and in particular consider these specific questions:

- Does the manufacturer arrange collection from you for the repair and delivery to you when the repair is completed, or are you expected to arrange that?

- Will the manufacturer arrange for repairs to be completed at your own premises?

- Is there a suggested turnaround time for repairs?

- Are there any elements of the laptop which are *not* covered by the warranty?

- Is there an opportunity to extend the warranty period or improve the conditions at the point of purchase? This may be cheaper than buying a new warranty at a later date.

Warranties and insurance

Laptop warranties

1 Check the warranty that came with your laptop.

2 If you need to complete a registration process to ensure the company has a record that you own the laptop, do it straight away to ensure the warranty is valid.

3 Keep copies of any registration numbers or documents which you need to send off to activate your warranty in a safe place with all your other household management documents.

Warranties and insurance (cont.)

Household insurance

1. Find your household insurance policy.

2. Check through it to find out if it covers loss or theft from outside the home and if it specifically includes or excludes computers.

3. Find out if you are required to list items over a certain value separately and decide whether to do this. You may need to pay an additional premium for the extra cover.

4. Be clear about what the policy actually covers and what types of damage it might cover.

Insurance

You may wish to consider insuring your laptop. It is possible to insure against losing your laptop or having it stolen, and even for some kinds of accidental damage.

Contact your household insurer to find out if they provide this kind of cover and check exactly what they do and don't cover. Do they cover damage outside the home or theft from outside the home, for example? If they don't, how expensive is it to add this to the insurance policy?

There are companies which specialise in providing laptop cover and you could research their conditions and pricing arrangements in addition to checking your home insurance policy to find out where and how you can get the best and most comprehensive deal.

If you already have access to a computer you can use the Internet to research this, but be wary of taking out any insurance policy if you are not already aware of the company offering it. The first rule of buying anything at all on the Internet is that you need to be sure you can trust the seller. So you will need to check out any companies you think you may buy from as thoroughly as you can before buying to make sure they are legitimate and able to meet any requirements of any policies they may offer.

Ask friends, family, work colleagues and others for their advice and experience. Ask them what they like and dislike about their own laptop, what they will look for next time they buy, what they thought they would need but actually don't find very useful.

You can also use the Internet and magazines to find reviews of the many different laptops that are available. A friend will probably let you use their computer for a little research of this kind.

At the end of this book you will find a list of laptop companies in the UK and their websites.

 Choosing a brand

2

Try before you buy

There are so many aspects of a laptop that are about how the machine feels to you – the screen size, the keyboard and the size and weight – that it can be a very good idea to try before you make a buying decision to make sure that everything feels just right for you.

There are two key methods you could use.

- Go into shops that sell computers and practise with those on display. Be serious about this. Type some real text to see how the keyboard feels to you. Seriously consider the screen size and decide whether it will be appropriate for all of your needs. Pick up the laptop and see if its weight is OK for you. Imagine that when you carry it around you may be carrying other things too, at the very least its power supply but maybe also a mouse, some other extra equipment and maybe other things too such as books or paperwork.
- Speak to friends who own computers. Ask about the pros and cons of their choices, and ask if you can try them out to see how they feel to you.

Points to consider

- If possible it is a good idea to try out a laptop before you buy it, just to make sure it is comfy to use and meets your requirements.
- See how easy it is to lift and carry. Will it fit in your bag? Can you carry it for as long as you want to? Consider the extra weight and volume the power supply adds.
- Is the screen really large enough for your needs?
- Try the keyboard. Is it comfortable to use?
- Check the positioning of all the connectors. Are they going to work well for you when you come to connect external devices?

Choosing the right laptop

3

Introduction

There are many different factors to weigh up when choosing a laptop. In this chapter we outline the most important ones, explaining the variations you might see and offering some tips to help you decide what suits you best.

We look at both internal features like the processor, hard drive and memory, and external features like the overall laptop size, its keyboard, screen size and operating system.

At the very end of the chapter there is a checklist you can use to help you get down on paper the basic specifications you think you need. It might be useful to turn to the checklist now to get familiar with it, and then as you progress through this chapter to mark up your ideal specifications.

Jargon buster

Operating system: the main software engine of any computer. The operating system includes facilities that allow software to run and share computer resources, allow hardware to run, and allow users to interact with software and hardware via the user interface.

What you'll do

Looks appealing

Types of laptop

Mobile broadband

Choosing between size and portability

Screens

Operating systems

The processor

RAM memory

Hard drive size

Graphics capability

The keyboard

Other buttons

Touchpads and sticks

Touch screens

Fingerprint recognition

Webcams

Built-in lighting

Ports and connectors

USB ports

Laptop buyer's checklist

Looks appealing

Laptop sellers can spend a lot of time trying to make their laptops look different from the others. This is partly done to help differentiate one product from another, and partly to draw potential customers to a laptop because of its appearance.

Elements that can be part of this design process include:

- the finish of the outer casing which can range from a slate type effect through to shiny metallic designs.

- bright colours are increasingly used for the outer casing rather than the traditional black, grey and silver. (You even occasionally see materials such as leather or faux leather being used. Computer manufacturer Asus recently launched a laptop with a bamboo lid; bamboo is a more environmentally friendly material than plastic or metal. It certainly lends the laptop a distinctive look.)

- curving of the casing to avoid a 'boxy' appearance.

- the use of lighting in various colours around buttons and other areas to show they are active; white and blue are particularly popular.

- the positioning and design of speakers and other buttons and connectors.

- where and how logos are displayed.

Part of the process of choosing the right laptop for your needs is not to get too carried away with making a selection based on just its looks. In fact, while you may be initially drawn to a laptop by how it looks, this is far less important than its overall specifications, how easy you find it to use and how well made it is. That last point is especially important. Laptops can take a lot of knocks, and ideally you want one with a solid and robust build.

Laptops come in all shapes and sizes, with the largest being too large for many people to want to carry around regularly, and the smallest almost small enough to fit into a pocket.

A number of terms are used to describe the different types of laptop and help tie them to types of user. Some of the terms used refer primarily to size, others to general capabilities and specifications. They can be of help in thinking about what kind of laptop is most suitable to your needs.

In the last chapter we helped you work out what kind of user you are. So now it is possible one of the descriptions below will seem entirely appropriate to your needs. Don't worry if it doesn't, though. As you read on you will learn more about different laptop features that will help you make a good choice.

Desktop replacement

Can be large in size and offer screens up to 17 inches (and sometimes larger) measured across the diagonal. They are not easy to carry around, but are not designed to be moved very far or very often. The emphasis is more on providing a good keyboard and large screen as well as solid internal components.

3

For your information

This laptop can be described as a desktop replacement. It is made by Samsung and is the R700. Its screen measures 17 inches across the diagonal and it weighs 3.2 kg.

Types of laptop (cont.)

Small and/or lightweight

Designed to be carried from place to place yet still offer a very strong range of features, small and lightweight laptops are a popular choice for many as they represent a good compromise between features, performance and portability.

Ultraportable

Generally weighing no more than 1.5 kg, ultraportable laptops are designed to be very small and light. The compromises that are made to meet this key requirement include small screen and keyboard. Optical drives are sometimes sacrificed too.

For your information

This laptop fits into the ultraportable category. It is Fujitsu Siemens' Lifebook P7230. Its screen measures just 10.6 inches across the diagonal and it weighs 1.25 kg.

Budget

Budget laptops by their very definition tend to lack the latest features but can still offer a strong range of capabilities and prove very useful for the average home or office user. They tend to be neither very large (desktop replacement sized) nor very small (ultraportable) but instead to be mid-sized, typically having screens that measure 15.4 inches across the diagonal.

Gaming

Gaming laptops tend to have large hard drives, large screens and superb graphics performance. They can be expensive because they bring together sophisticated and top of the range components including the latest (and fastest) processors and large screens. They tend not to be very portable.

Business

Business users fall into many camps with many different computing requirements, but an important generality is that they need to carry their laptops from place to place. Thus business laptops tend to be relatively light and small. They can have some high-end features like the latest processors and built in 3G communications, but tend to lack some of the features that home users or consumers might like such as brightly designed casings and shiny screen coatings (intended to enhance clarity).

Tablet PCs

Tablet PCs come in two types: a 'slate' style laptop without a keyboard and a more ordinary looking laptop with a screen which swivels and lays down flat on the keyboard facing outermost. Tablet PCs have touch screens that either require a special stylus (which is provided), or are fingertip sensitive. They include features like handwriting recognition and are designed to be used at least for part of the time by being held in one hand as you might hold a pad of paper or clip-board.

3

For your information

This is a tablet PC. In this kind of laptop the screen swivels round so you can lay it flat on the keyboard facing outwards.

Types of laptop (cont.)

Rugged

Some laptops are designed specifically to be used in challenging – often outdoor – circumstances and have a very solid outer casing as well as special protection for more delicate internal parts. This adds to weight but increases toughness. There are sets of international standards for rugged laptops. Rugged laptops can be very expensive because of their specialised components. They are generally not an option the home, college or office-based user would need to consider.

Mini-laptops or netbooks

Different to the budget laptops mentioned earlier, a new class of low-cost computer has started to emerge.

Manufacturer Asus has spearheaded the genre with its Eee PC, a class of computer which in its first incarnation ran the Linux operating system but now also comes in versions which run Microsoft Windows. Asus has been joined by many others, with most of the leading players having a netbook in their range.

The computers are typically very small, with screens measuring not more than 10 inches across the diagonal. They have low-end specifications but for many users could be suitable for everyday computing. They could suit others as a second computer. They are designed for low power consumption, and spring partly from projects to develop low-cost computers for nations that lack the financial and technical facilities for traditional computing and partly from developments in computing for the education sector.

3

For your information ⓘ

The netbook is a new and fast-growing genre of low-cost notebook. Asus is regarded as having started the trend for these computers, with its Eee PC range.

Types of laptop (cont.)

Ultra mobile PC or UMPC

This is a relatively new format of computer and there are very few on the market at the moment. The UMPC does not have a built-in keyboard and so arguably is not a laptop at all. However, as it is designed for mobile and portable computing it is worth discussing here.

Typically a UMPC is a screen-only device though it is possible to plug in a separate keyboard should you need one. The screens on UMPCs generally measure no more than 8 inches across the diagonal and are touch-sensitive.

The UMPC is a Microsoft concept, and as we write UMPCs tend to run a Microsoft operating system, though this may change in the future. They run a complete version of the operating system and so you should be able to install any software you can use on a laptop or desktop computer. However, their small screens and lack of keyboard make them unsuitable for some tasks.

Companies currently active with UMPCs available include Samsung and Asus.

Over the past year or so mobile broadband has become increasingly popular. The term refers to using your laptop to access the mobile phone network at fast speeds in order to access data such as your email or that on the Internet while on the move. The UK's main mobile network operators, 3, O2, Orange, T-Mobile and Vodafone, all have mobile broadband services in operation.

There are two ways in which you might get mobile broadband on your laptop:

■ Via an integrated SIM card. Some laptops, including a number of netbooks, have a slot for a SIM card. The advantage of this is that the mobile data access is built into the laptop without any need for you to add anything to it.

■ Via a 'dongle'. This is a small device, that looks like a USB flash memory stick and fits into a USB slot on your laptop. A SIM card then fits into this. It will be a 'plug and play' device, which means it will install its software automatically and work without any more intervention by you. The advantage of this is that you could use it with any computer to get access to the mobile Internet. However, you will need to carry it along with your laptop.

If you are considering a laptop with a mobile broadband make sure you look at the financial angles. The network operators all have offers which bundle mobile broadband with a laptop for a monthly tariff. They also offer their mobile broadband dongles on a monthly tariff. You may find it is more cost effective for you to take one option or the other. Compare the 'all-in' cost with the alternative of buying the laptop and dongle separately. Take into account the length of the contract, whether the laptop on offer really meets your current needs, whether you are happy to take a contract for the required period, and whether you might want to change your laptop before the contract period is up.

Mobile broadband

Choosing mobile broadband

1 Decide if there is an operator you prefer for your mobile broadband service.

2 Visit the websites of all the operators and compare their prices and what they offer.

3 You might find it useful to make notes from the websites as operators present their information in different ways.

4 Make sure you have an accessible and convenient USB slot into which to fit a USB dongle and make a note to yourself that this will be in use and so unavailable for other items.

5 Be aware that mobile broadband dongles can be large, and if two USB slots are close together a dongle may obscure access to the second slot.

3

Choosing between size and portability

Laptops can range in weight from around 1 kg to more than 7 kg. This is a vast range and the average weight sitting between these extremes is around the 3 kg mark. Larger laptops benefit from bigger screens and keyboards, but they are inevitably less easy to carry around than smaller, lighter ones.

Some of the smallest and lightest laptops do not have a built-in optical drive. Sometimes one may be included within the price of the laptop, sometimes you will need to buy one as an extra item if you want it. Either way, you will need to connect it to the laptop when you want to use it.

An external optical drive is an extra thing to carry around and so adds to overall bulk and weight. If you choose not to carry the external optical drive for any reason you won't be able to access anything stored on an optical disk, for example DVD movies, music, software or data stored on a CD.

The compromise between size and portability is a matter of personal choice. Considering how often you are likely to want to carry your laptop and how far it will travel should help you make a good choice. If you are only likely to want to move your laptop around in your home, for example, then a larger one with a bigger screen might seem more alluring than if you need to carry a laptop around fairly frequently.

Important

Be aware that if you choose a mobile broadband option the speeds quoted will be the maximum speeds attainable. You may not actually experience these speeds everywhere, and what you do experience will depend on what the network offers where you happen to be. It is most important that you check the speeds available in the location you are most likely to do most of your computing – probably that will be at home – to ensure that you are aware of the service you should expect.

Timesaver tip

If you are certain you will want to carry your laptop between locations you'll need a bag to carry it in. Some laptops come with a carrying case. While this is undoubtedly handy, it is probably not important enough to sway your buying decision between one laptop and the next. There are many carrying cases available, including briefcase types, messenger bags and rucksacks, and many are relatively inexpensive.

The physical size of a laptop screen is measured diagonally across opposite corners, in inches. There is an amazing variety of screen sizes ranging from as little as 7 inches right up to 17 inches and even more.

Wide screens and aspect ratios

The rise of widescreen in home TVs has been mirrored by a similar development in computers. Traditionally, laptops (like desktop computers) always had screens wider than they were tall, with a relationship between width and height of 4 to 3. This is generally written 4:3.

With the increase in multimedia uses for modern computers there has been a parallel rise in wide screens. This is seen in both desktop monitors and laptops. Typically today the 4:3 aspect ratio is waning and being replaced with an aspect ratio of 16:10 or 16:9. Both of these aspect ratios stretch the width further than 4:3, making screens considerably wider than they are tall.

There are benefits to having this wide format for both leisure and professional users. You can watch widescreen movies in comfort, but also, if you are keen on using your computer for text or graphics production, it is easier to have two working windows open at once and sitting side by side. If you like to use spreadsheets and make them with lots of horizontal rows of information, you can see more information at once without the need to scroll. If you are a games player, the wider and larger the screen, the more 'immersive' your experience of a game is likely to be.

Pixels

At the heart of all this are pixels, the tiny dots of colour which make up the images on a computer screen. Pixel sizes actually change with the overall screen size, but this level of detail is not usually made apparent in computer specifications. Instead you are given the actual number of pixels a screen can display in both width and height. This is known as the 'screen resolution'.

Screens

What size screen do you need?

1 Think about the kinds of activities you might do with your laptop as this will affect the most appropriate screen size.

2 The kinds of tasks that might benefit from a larger screen include: watching DVDs, streaming video from the Internet such as timeshifted television, editing photos and playing games.

3 Think about the trade-off between the larger screens and portability. Big screens mean big laptops which are heavy to carry. Decide where the best point of compromise is for you.

4 If you really need a large screen but also want a highly portable laptop, consider buying an external monitor.

3

Screens (cont.)

Below are some of the common pixel ratios you will find in laptops.

Number of pixels (width × height), also known as 'screen resolution'	Shorthand term	Widescreen or standard
1024 × 768	XGA	Standard
1280 × 800	WXGA	Widescreen
1280 × 1024	SXGA	Standard
1400 × 1050	SXGA+	Standard
1680 × 1050	WSXGA+	Widescreen
1600 × 1200	UXGA	Standard
1920 × 1200	WUXGA	Widescreen

A laptop might have three different types of information about pixels associated with it:

- The maximum 'native' resolution. This is the maximum resolution your laptop can display using its built-in screen management software. It is probably the ideal resolution for using the laptop. Typically it will be possible to set several lower resolutions should you want to do so.

- The maximum resolution that can be sent to an external monitor. It is usually possible to plug an external monitor into a laptop computer and use it to display screen contents. Some laptops can produce output to a higher resolution on external monitors than they can internally. This could be very useful if you want a small laptop for carrying around but want to use a larger screen with greater display area when you are at your desk.

- Interpolated resolution. You don't often see this on laptops, but when you do it means that the screen can display a higher resolution than its hardware caters for thanks to software manipulation of the images displayed. Interpolated higher resolutions can be a little difficult to read, coming across as 'fuzzy' to the eye, and generally are not suited to frequent use.

Did you know?

You can change the display resolution on your laptop.

Screen coatings

Many laptop screens have a special coating which is designed to help make them clearer and sharper to read. Typically these coatings appear on consumer grade laptops. Different manufacturers have different names for the technology they use.

While some people find these coatings enhance their computing experience, others are less sure of the benefits. Certainly, the coatings can be rather reflective, so that working with a light source behind you can mean that the screen takes on a mirror-like quality reflecting your surroundings back at you.

Timesaver tip

If you are deciding between a laptop with and one without such a coating, it might be a good idea to see examples of both before making a decision. You should be able to do this in any high-street store that sells laptop computers. Bear in mind that if you examine a laptop in a store you might not see the full effect of its reflective coating under the lights in the store. Ideally you need to be able to try it in a situation with a light source behind you to see whether the reflective coating is an issue for you. This could be easier said than done!

Change screen resolution in Windows 7

1. Click Start then click Control Panel.

2. Choose Adjust the screen resolution.

3. Click the Resolution drop down box. All the available resolutions for your screen will be shown.

4. Drag the pointer to the resolution you require, then click OK.

5. You will be asked in a new window if you want to keep the display settings. Click Keep Changes if you are happy or Revert to stick with the old settings.

3

Operating systems

Choosing an operating system

1. If you want the choice between as wide a range of laptops as possible then you will need to opt for a Microsoft operating system.

2. Linux is not an ideal choice for anyone new to computing as it can be somewhat technical to get to grips with and finding help will be less easy than it is with Windows or the Mac operating system.

3. The Mac operating system is only available on laptops from Apple. The best way to see the full range and try them out is to visit an Apple store near you.

An operating system is a key component of any computer regardless of whether it is a laptop or a desktop machine. The operating system is a piece of software which ensures that a computer runs efficiently and that you are able to use it. It has several tasks including:

- Providing a way for you the user to interact with the computer and its software and hardware. This is referred to as the 'user interface' and it is what you see when you switch on your computer. Whenever you do anything on your computer, from running an application to changing the screen display settings or installing a new application, you are using the user interface.

- Enabling the sharing of computer resources, for example sharing the internal memory of the computer between different software applications and sharing hardware resources such as a printer between different software applications that allow you to print.

- Providing information that allows software and hardware to function properly and to interact efficiently.

Just like desktop PCs, laptops come with an operating system already installed when you buy them. The most popular and frequently seen operating systems are Microsoft Windows and the Mac OS. It is also possible to install Linux, a free operating system, onto laptops and to buy some laptops with Linux pre-installed.

Microsoft Windows

As we write there are several versions of Windows in existence. The newest version is known as Windows 7. It comes in several different varieties – the ones you are most likely to come across are Windows 7 Home Premium, Windows 7 Professional and Windows 7 Ultimate.

The versions have a different range of features, as you'll see in the table.

Feature	Windows 7 Home Premium	Windows 7 Professional	Windows 7 Ultimate
Improve desktop navigation	✓	✓	✓
Start programs faster and more easily and quickly. Find the documents you use most often	✓	✓	✓
Make your Web experience faster, easier and safer than ever with Internet Explorer 8	✓	✓	✓
Watch many of your favourite TV shows for free when and where you want with Internet TV	✓	✓	✓
Easily create a home network and connect your PCs to a printer with HomeGroup	✓	✓	✓
Run many Windows XP productivity programs in Windows XP mode		✓	✓
Connect to company networks easily and more securely with Domain Join		✓	✓
In addition to full system Backup and Restore found in all editions, you can back up to a home or business network		✓	✓
Help protect data on your PC and portable storage devices with BitLocker			✓
Work in the language of your choice and choose between any of 35 languages			✓

?

Did you know?

Windows 7 is Microsoft's most recent operating system for PCs.

3

Operating systems (cont.)

The earlier version, Windows Vista, also comes in several different versions: Home Basic, Home Premium, Business, Enterprise and Ultimate. The two varieties you are most likely to come across are Home Premium and Business. There are differences between the two. Some elements more appropriate to home users are missing from the Business version, and vice versa.

You may also come across the previous Microsoft Windows operating system, Windows XP. As we write this is still being offered on many netbooks.

Windows XP comes in two laptop versions, Professional and Home. There is also a tablet PC edition which includes special features to make use of the touch screens on tablet PCs and Media Centre edition for Media Centre PCs (PCs designed to be used as home entertainment hubs).

Microsoft issues sporadic major upgrades to its operating systems. The latest upgrade to Windows XP is Service Pack 3 while Windows Vista has had two service packs issued. These service packs include all the small upgrades which are issued regularly by Microsoft such as security fixes.

Timesaver tip

If you choose to buy your laptop second-hand then you are more likely to find it runs Windows Vista or Windows XP rather than the new Windows 7.

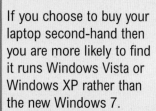

Important

Both Microsoft Windows and the Mac OS can be updated by download over your Internet connection, and the process can be set to run automatically.

For your information

You can learn more about Windows 7 at *http://www.microsoft.com/windows/windows-7*.

You can find out more about Microsoft's operating system and upgrades at *www.microsoft.com/uk*.

The Mac OS

Apple's Mac computers have their own operating system. The very latest version is known as Snow Leopard. When its predecessor Mac OS 10 was announced it added more than 300 features to the previous version.

For your information

You can find out more about the Mac OS X Snow Leopard at *http://www.apple.com/macosx/*

Timesaver tip

Before installing a major operating system update check the Internet to find out if there are any problems with it. Sometimes it is not advisable to be first in the queue for such things. Computers are very complex machines, and they have to manage a huge variety of set-ups that suit different people's needs. This can mean that major updates are not always stable on every computer to which they are installed. Sometimes it is wise to wait a bit for problems to be ironed out.

Linux

Linux is not as well known as the Mac OS or Microsoft Windows, but an increasing number of computing enthusiasts choose it as their preferred operating system. Usually users install it themselves as it is only rarely an option when buying a laptop. The exception to this is that some small, low-cost netbooks run Linux. It is chosen because it helps keep the computer's overall cost low.

Timesaver tip

Before updating your operating system to a newer version you should check on the system requirements to make sure your computer meets the needs. You could find, for example, if you don't have enough RAM memory, that an upgraded operating system runs very slowly.

3

Operating systems (cont.)

For your information

You can find out more about Linux at *http://www.linux.org/*

You pronounce Linux by emphasising the 'i' – try saying 'line-ucks'.

The Linux operating system is completely free and is based on a core or 'kernel' which is the centre of a number of different versions or 'distributions' of the software. Some distributions of Linux are charged for, and technically in these cases you are paying for the packaging and distribution service as well as extra elements of software, but not for the kernel Linux software itself.

Linux is arguably more suitable for enthusiasts who are confident with installing a new operating system from scratch than those who are inexperienced or who just want to take their computer out of its box and start to use it productively.

The processor is the core 'brain' of your laptop. It is where the thinking gets done, where things get worked out before they are delivered to the screen.

When you click something the processor works out what you want to do and gets it done. When you type a letter in a document the processor works out what letter you want and puts that on the screen; when you play a video file or a music file the processor takes the data from your hard drive and turns it into the video you see on screen.

Processors are measured by their speed and this is given as a rating in gigahertz (GHz). This is basically a count of the number of processes that can be carried out in a second. A 2.0GHz processor can carry out 2 billion processes every second. The higher the number, the faster the speed. So a 1.6GHz processor is not as fast as a 2.0GHz processor.

Cache is a special kind of memory that can store information so that it can be accessed quickly by the computer. For example, the cache might store some information it gets from the hard drive in anticipation of you needing it. It is faster to read and write to this kind of memory than to the hard drive, so using cache memory can help speed up a computer. Modern processors incorporate cache memory to help boost their performance.

In recent times multi-core processors have started to be popular in both desktop and laptop computers. Dual core processors are currently popular in laptops. Dual core processors have two main processing units rather than the one that used to be found in all computers. Having two processing units means that data can be dealt with much more quickly, again providing a speed boost to any laptop.

The processor

3

The processor (cont.)

Choosing a processor

1 Your selected laptop may come with several different processor options. What you choose will affect the price and capabilities.

2 More capable processors are more expensive, but you might not need to go to the top of the range.

3 If your main requirements are word processing and browsing the Web you may be fine with the lowest specification processor in the model of laptop you have chosen.

4 If you want to do tasks that need the computer to do a lot of work, such as playing games or watching DVDs, then a more capable processor might be the ideal choice.

How fast is fast enough?

The answer to that question depends on what you want to do with your computer. If you only want to write documents and do email, then you needn't look for a fast processor. If you want to play fast-paced games, or are interested in manipulating large graphics files, maybe a faster processor is better suited to your needs.

For your information

The processor is the part of your laptop often referred to as the 'brain'. It carries out instructions which ensure your computer does what you ask it to.

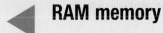

The RAM, or Random Access Memory, is where the computer keeps everything that is currently in use. If an application is opened it is stored in the RAM. The document you are writing is stored in the RAM too. When you save the document, it is copied to the hard drive, but everything you create between one 'save' and the next is kept in RAM memory. So are various bits of software that automatically run when you turn on your computer.

RAM memory is thus crucial to any laptop. It is the 'working memory' where the key computing activity takes place. If you don't have enough of it your laptop can start to run very slowly indeed, and become difficult to work with.

Operating systems and applications generally specify an amount of RAM they need to work in. Both a 'recommended' and a minimum amount are often quoted. It is most effective to have the recommended amount available, and more if possible.

When you are first looking at buying a laptop you may find yourself weighing up the pros and cons of spending money on a faster processor or more RAM. We would suggest you opt for the RAM. Choosing 2GB of RAM memory rather than 1GB can give your laptop more of a speed boost than adding a few gigahertz of speed by buying a faster processor. This is especially the case if you expect to work with lots of large files such as photographs or movie footage.

3

Hard drive size

The hard drive is the central storage area of your laptop. It is where all your data and software are kept. Fill it up and you will be in trouble as you'll need to find another place to store data or consider an upgrade (see Chapter 5).

Laptop hard drives come in a range of capacities. Typically today you will find laptops offering hard drives of any size between about 100GB and 500GB. That is a huge size range, and gauging how much storage you are likely to need is tricky, especially if you aren't sure what kinds of uses you will put your laptop to. The best advice here is to think big and buy the largest hard drive you can afford.

If you find yourself unexpectedly interested in making and editing home movies, for example, you will find a larger hard drive is a real boon.

Choosing a hard drive size

1 Laptops come with a range of different hard drive sizes. It is difficult to upgrade the hard drive so it is important to make the right choice at the start.

2 Will you want to keep a lot of photos and videos? Then you need a larger hard drive.

3 Will you mostly be storing documents and email? Then you probably need a smaller hard drive.

4 If you have the funds, buy the largest hard drive you can afford for your chosen laptop so that it will take longer to fill it. You will get better value in the long term.

A laptop's graphics are managed by special hardware. In a laptop the graphics management could be built into the main system or it could be managed by a separate graphics card.

If your main aims with your laptop include things like word processing, Web browsing, email and maybe a little spreadsheet work, then graphics which are managed by the main system are fine. But some types of activity can require a lot of graphics work. If, for example, you are interested in viewing a lot of video either by playing DVDs on your laptop or editing your own home-shot video, then you may find a good dedicated graphics card is more able to cope than graphics management which is built onto the main system. Similarly, if you are very interested in playing games on your laptop a separate dedicated graphics card could be a real boon.

For your information

You may see the choice referred to as 'discrete' versus 'integrated' graphics where discrete refers to having a separate graphics card and integrated refers to graphics being managed by the main system..

◀ **Graphics capability**

Graphics capability

1. Graphics are managed either by a separate graphics card or are integrated into the main system.

2. Decide if you want to do a lot of rich media activity such as: playing games; streaming media from the Internet; playing DVDs; editing and watching your own home-shot videos.

3. If you do then a laptop with a separate graphics card might be the best choice for you.

3

The keyboard

Alongside the screen the keyboard is probably the most important aspect of your laptop from an everyday use point of view. You will use the keyboard every time you want to do anything at all, be it write an official letter, play a music CD, draw up a budgeting spreadsheet, write an email, do some Web research or even download photos from your digital camera. So it is very important that the keyboard is right for you. There are several factors to consider.

Key size

Many laptops are described as having 'full sized' keys. However, the smaller the overall size of the laptop, the less likely it will be that it can accommodate a keyboard as you might be used to seeing it in relation to a desktop PC.

The tops of the keys – the bits you tap with your fingers – may be 'full sized' on many laptops, but the spacing between keys may be minimal, and overall the area allocated to the keyboard, and in particular its width, may be less than you are used to with a desktop.

On smaller laptops the tops of keys are likely to be less than full sized, simply because the amount of space available is reduced.

If you have larger hands the keyboards on smaller laptops may be too cramped for you to use comfortably. If you are a touch-typist you may find smaller laptop keyboards take some getting used to, and you could even find that they remain less speedy to use than a standard keyboard in the long term.

Key travel

When you press a key on a keyboard it is pushed down and makes a connection with the circuitry that records it has been pressed. The degree to which it depresses is known as the 'travel'.

Some people like a lot of travel on keys, others are happy with less. This is a personal matter, but having too much or not enough travel can affect your typing efficiency. The only way to really know if a keyboard suits you is to try it.

Layout

The A to Z letters, also known as the QWERTY keys, have the same layout on a laptop keyboard as they do on a desktop. In addition you can expect to find many of the other keys in familiar places. The Enter key, Caps Lock, Shift and space bar, for example, will all be in familiar locations. However, some of the keys can vary in size and this can be an issue for some users. For example, a very short space bar could cause problems for an experienced touch-typist who is used to a desktop keyboard. The same can be said for an Enter key which is smaller than usually found on a desktop keyboard.

In addition, other elements of a laptop keyboard may be less familiar as non-QWERTY key layouts can vary from one laptop to another. However, we can make some general points.

Separate number pads

Desktop keyboards tend to have a separate calculator style number pad. There is only room for this in the very largest of laptops. Two approaches are taken to accommodating a number pad. Firstly, laptops generally have a row of numbers sitting above the top QWERTY row. Secondly, in addition many laptops have a second set of number keys available in combination with a function key for single presses or a Num

3

For your information

The keyboard is very important. It needs to be well made and have keys which are large enough for you to use without feeling cramped.

The keyboard (cont.)

Lock key for continuous use. These get close to the calculator style layout of desktop keyboards and often include the basic mathematical symbols that a desktop number pad also offers (+, −, * (multiplication), / (division), . (decimal point)).

Control keys

Insert, Delete, Page up, Page down, Home, End, up, down, left and right are control keys and are usually found in two separate banks on a laptop keyboard. Some may require the use of a function key to activate them.

The up, down, left and right control keys are often ranged in what is called an 'inverted T' and arrows indicate the direction of movement when you press each key. They can be used to move the cursor around in a window containing text and can also sometimes have second functions when used with the Fn key.

Also, the 'inverted T' keys can have additional functions. For example, in Microsoft Word, pressing the Alt and F keys together will open the file menu, then using the 'arrow' keys will move you through the menu options, while the Enter key makes a selection. In fact, this is the same as the system used on a desktop keyboard.

Timesaver tip

If you are changing from a desktop keyboard to a laptop one, or need to use both types (e.g. because you have a desktop computer at work and a laptop at home), then you may find the differences take a little getting used to. This may be the case if you use a lot of keyboard shortcuts instead of using the mouse. On the other hand, some people have no trouble at all using the two systems. If you are in doubt it might be a good idea to try the keyboard on a laptop you like for some serious typing before you make a buying decision.

Important

If you are a touch-typist you may want to check that all the keys are where you expect them to be and of an appropriate size as slight variations can take a little getting used to at first.

The keyboard (cont.)

Get to know the keyboard

1. Place your fingers on the keys and try tapping them slowly as if you were typing. Do they feel comfortable? Do they depress enough for you? Are they too close together, too far apart, or just right?

2. Try reaching for the shift keys and the other keys outside the keyboard. Do they feel as though they are in intuitive locations? Are they easy to reach?

3. Can you see all the keys you are likely to need?

4. Look at any keys which are extra to the keyboard. Are they useful or not? Do those that start applications such as email software or the Web browser look useful? Are there keys for features you'll need a lot such as volume control? Or do the extra keys seem unnecessary to you?

3

Other buttons

Many laptops have additional keys or buttons beyond those we have mentioned so far. These can offer access to a range of features and can help make it easy and fast to get around the laptop.

Examples include:

- **Power saving keys**: these can selectively turn off elements of the laptop in order to save power and extend battery life.

- **Wireless keys**: these can turn the Wi-Fi and Bluetooth modules on and off as a power saving and security feature.

- **Media control keys**: like the forward, back, pause and play buttons on a CD player these can be used to control music or DVD playback.

- **Internet key**: this can be used to start your Web browser ready for an online session.

- **Email key**: this can be used to start your email software ready for you to send and receive messages.

- **Volume keys**: available so that you can easily control the system volume or mute it completely. You may also find a wheel for controlling volume, or in some cases a touch sensitive strip along which you can drag a finger.

- **User programmable keys**: some laptops offer one or more keys you can program to launch applications you use frequently.

Jargon buster

Bluetooth: a wireless technology designed typically to connect just two devices together for a short period of time, and over a short distance. For example, a mobile phone and a wireless headset or a laptop computer and a mobile phone or smartphone.

Wi-Fi: the name given to a wireless communications standard widely used for wireless networking. Also known as 802.11.

3

Touchpads and sticks

Get to know the touchpad

1 Place your hands on the keyboard and rest a thumb on the touchpad, or place a finger on the touchpad.

2 Move your thumb or finger around and watch as the cursor on screen moves in synchronisation.

3 Put the cursor over an application icon on the screen.

4 Tap the touchpad twice and the application will open.

5 Look at the right and bottom edges of the touchpad. Are there any markings? If so they indicate that there are 'scroll zones'. There may be scroll zones even if there are no markings.

6 Open an application such as the Web browser.

7 Place the cursor in the application window and if the view extends beyond the bottom of the window run a finger down the right side of the touchpad. If there is a scroll zone the content should scroll down. Scroll up and the content should follow.

We have already noted one way of moving the cursor around – the 'arrow keys' on your keyboard. But when you want to move the screen pointer, as you would do with a mouse on a desktop computer, you need a different system.

The most commonly occurring system for this type of cursor control on a laptop computer is the touchpad. This is a flat pad that sits beneath the keyboard and responds when you pass a fingertip over it, causing the on-screen cursor to move around in sync with your fingertip.

Some touchpads incorporate a 'scrollbar' system. This allows you to drag a finger along a vertical and horizontal edge of the touchpad in order to scroll through documents. This can be useful for Web browsing or moving through longer documents. Others incorporate different systems, such as a rocker button that sits in between the left and right mouse buttons. You can use this rocker button for scrolling vertically through longer documents, though not for horizontal scrolling.

Another popular system for cursor control is the 'stick'. Usually nestled between the G, H and B keys this is in effect a miniature joystick which you can use to drag the cursor around on the screen.

Whichever system a notebook has, and some manage to combine both stick and touchpad, there will also be at least two buttons which emulate the left and right buttons on a mouse.

If a laptop has both a touchpad and a stick then it may have two sets of mouse buttons, one beneath the touchpad and one above it or immediately beneath the space bar. These are present so that you can find the pair that work most ergonomically for you depending on whether you choose to use mostly the touchpad or mostly the stick.

8 Repeat this test when the content of a window extends off the right or left edge, this time running a finger along the bottom edge of the touchpad. If there is a scroll zone the content should scroll horizontally.

Get to know the touchstick

1 Some laptops have a small stick sitting between the G, H and B keys. You can move this with a fingertip to move the cursor around on screen.

2 If there is a touchstick there might also be a pair of buttons immediately beneath the space bar.

3 You can use these buttons like left and right mouse buttons.

For your information

Some laptops have both a touchpad and a trackstick. In this case there is often a second set of mouse buttons sitting immediately beneath the space bar, so you can use these easily with the trackstick.

3

Touch screens

Did you know?

Some laptops have touch sensitive screens. These might respond to finger taps or to a special stylus.

Touch sensitive screens are most often found in tablet PCs, but it is also possible to find them in some ordinary laptops. There are two types of touchscreen – 'active' and 'passive'.

Active screens require a special stylus to be used. Most often found in tablet PCs the stylus resides in a housing on the laptop itself. The stylus looks like a plastic pen and allows you to control the cursor, tap menus and even write direct onto the screen and have your handwriting turned into text you can edit using the keyboard.

A key advantage of an active screen is that you can touch it with a finger and not affect it. A key disadvantage is that if you lose the special stylus you will need to purchase a replacement.

Passive screens are responsive to a range of objects. There are two types of passive screen, both of which are actually governed by electrical current rather than by touch.

In 'resistive' screen types a finger tip or other object pushes two layers of material together and this registers an electrical contact between the layers. The computer's processor interprets the coordinates of the 'touch' and ensures the required action is performed.

In 'capacitive' touch screens an electrical charge runs through the surface layer of the screen. When you touch the screen with a fingertip the charge in the layer changes, and again the place of touch is registered and the required action performed. This kind of touch screen needs to be tapped with a finger or some other object that can conduct electricity. The charge is exceptionally low – users don't notice it at all!

Fingerprint recognition has started to appear in laptop computers with increasing frequency over the past few years. It is designed to help keep the contents of a computer secure and accessible only to the person with a fingerprint recognised by the laptop.

A reader is located somewhere on the laptop. Often it is somewhere on the keyboard area, but that is by no means a hard and fast rule and on tablet PCs it is more likely to be on the screen area so that it can be found when the screen is uppermost and the keyboard is covered. To make the fingerprint recognition work, you need to 'enrol' your chosen finger, which is done using software that is pre-installed onto the laptop.

Did you know?

A fingerprint scanner lets you log onto your laptop by sweeping a finger pad across the scanner.

3

Webcams

Built-in webcams are becoming more and more common. These are tiny cameras designed primarily to help you take advantage of increasingly popular Internet-based video calling. One or sometimes two microphones are also built in, so that voice can be captured as well as moving images.

These cameras are usually located above the screen, where it is easy for them to frame your face with the laptop sitting on a desk.

Webcams can have a range of features including the following:

- **Face tracking**: the webcam will automatically follow your face as you move around, keeping you in the centre of the frame as well as it can.
- **Automatic light adjustment**: the webcam will adjust itself to let in an appropriate amount of light for the prevailing conditions.
- **Automatic focus**: if you move closer to or further away from the laptop the camera will try to keep you in focus all the time.
- **Image and video capture**: webcams can often capture still image or video at a range of resolutions. Note though that most built-in webcams are relatively low resolution and they are not a substitute for a dedicated digital camera.

For your information

You would hardly notice it unless you were looking, but sitting above the screen on this laptop is a tiny webcam lens.

Webcams can also be used for security purposes. Some laptops have a system of face recognition-based login, in which part of the security control at login involves using the laptop's camera to recognise your face.

Get to know your webcam

1. Look above the screen. If your computer has a webcam that is where it will be.

2. Look on the screen. If you see a link for webcam software, double-click it to open it.

3. If there is no link to webcam software on the screen then look in the programs listing to find it. For example, in Windows 7 click Start then All Programs then look through the applications and folders for webcam software.

4. When the webcam software is running look for buttons which let you do the following: take a snapshot; shoot a video; set the webcam resolution.

5. You can use your webcam for video conferencing, but you will need additional software. Some might be included on your laptop, or you may need to add it. There are lots of alternatives including many that are free.

3

Built-in lighting

Some laptops have a built-in light above the screen. This can be used when the surrounding conditions are dark and you want to illuminate the keyboard to make typing easier.

The need for this is quite rare, and it is not found on many laptops, but it can be useful if you need to use your laptop in places that have darker surroundings, such as at night or on an airplane.

Laptops can have a whole host of ports and connectors situated around their four edges. These are designed to let you augment the features of your laptop by adding external devices, which are also known as peripherals. You can learn more about the types of peripherals which can be attached to a laptop in Chapter 7.

You may not find every type of connector on every laptop, but here is a list of those you may find:

- **USB**: a type of connector very widely used in a broad range of peripherals from printers to mobile music players.
- **VGA Out**: allows you to connect an external monitor with an analogue connector.
- **S-Video**: allows you to connect to a video recorder or TV.
- **Ethernet**: (also known as RJ-45) used to connect network devices such as a broadband modem or another computer.
- **Modem**: (also known as RJ-11) used to connect to a standard telephone socket to allow use of the laptop's internal modem over your phone line.
- **ExpressCard**: used to connect peripherals.
- **PC Card**: (also known as PCMCIA card) used to connect peripherals.
- **Card Reader**: used to connect a range of flash memory cards where the range supported will vary from laptop to laptop but can include compact flash, SD, MMC, xD, Memory Stick.
- **Firewire**: a connector used by some devices which need to transfer data to and from a computer.
- **Microphone**: a standard 3.5 mm connector for an external microphone.
- **Headphones**: a standard 3.5 mm connector for external headphones.
- **S/PDIF**: a 3.5 mm connector for digital music output.
- **HDMI**: (High Definition Multimedia Interface) digital video output.

Ports and connectors

Jargon buster

Broadband: the term used to describe modern high-speed Internet connections.

Card reader: a device for accessing flash memory cards such as SD, microSD, Memory Stick and xD picture cards. These are built into many laptops and can be added as a peripheral too.

Ethernet: a system for connecting devices such as two computers by wires. Laptops have Ethernet capability and a connection socket built into them.

3

USB ports ▶

Add a peripheral to your laptop

1. Take the peripheral you want to use, such as a mouse or keyboard.

2. Check the manual. In many cases peripherals are 'plug and play' which means you can simply plug them in and start to use them. However, some need additional software. Note the procedure for installing the peripheral.

3. Look at your laptop and locate the most appropriate USB port for your peripheral.

4. Follow the instructions in the manual. If there is no requirement to install any additional software, there will be a short wait while your laptop recognises the peripheral and sets it up.

Did you know?

Ports and connectors can sit on all four sides of a laptop.

Laptops can have as few as two USB ports, or can have three, four or even more. Don't just look at the total number available though. Look at the positions of the ports as well – this can be just as important as the overall number in terms of your ability to use them.

Proximity

If two USB ports are close together it might be difficult to use them both at once. Some peripherals have quite large connectors and it might be impossible to plug in two side by side.

Location

Are the ports nicely spread around the edges and back of the laptop? If they are all on one edge, how convenient is that for you? It is generally more convenient if they are spread around as it means you can more easily arrange your peripherals around your laptop.

USB hubs

You are not limited by the number of USB ports on your laptop. You can use a USB hub to add more ports easily. There is more on this in Chapter 7.

You can use this checklist to mark up the key characteristics of your ideal laptop. Then you can use it to help you weigh up the various options from different sellers. There is a list of sellers and their websites at the end of this book.

What format?
- Desktop replacement
- Small and lightweight
- Ultraportable
- Budget
- Gaming
- Business
- Tablet PC
- Rugged
- Mini-laptop or netbook
- Ultra mobile PC (UMPC)

What operating system?
- Microsoft Windows 7 Home Premium
- Microsoft Windows 7 Professional
- Microsoft Windows 7 Ultimate
- Microsoft Windows XP Home
- Microsoft Windows XP Professional
- Microsoft Windows Vista Business
- Microsoft Windows Vista Home
- Mac OS Snow Leopard
- Linux

Ports and connectors:
- USB ports (how many do you need?)
- VGA Out
- S-Video
- Ethernet (RJ-45)
- Modem (RJ-11)
- ExpressCard
- PC Card (also known as PCMCIA card)
- Card Reader for flash memory e.g. SD, MMC, xD, Memory Stick
- Firewire
- Microphone jack
- Headphones jack
- S/PDIF jack
- HDMI port

How much money?
- Less than £350
- £350 to £800
- More than £800

What processor?
I would prefer a processor in the following range:

....

Business or leisure?
- Primarily business
- Primarily leisure

Graphics capability:
- Separate graphics processor required?

Hard drive size:
- Less than 100GB
- 100GB to 250GB
- More than 250GB

Keyboard and cursor management:
- Need a separate number pad?
Keyboard size
- small
- medium
- large
Cursor control
- mini joystick
- trackpad

Additional features:
- webcam
- fingerprint scanner
- shortcut buttons for Internet, email and other features

Screen dimensions and characteristics:
- Less than 10 inches
- Around 12 inches
- 15 inches
- 17 inches
- More than 17 inches
- Need a touchscreen?
- Need a wide screen?

3

Communications and networking

Introduction

Like desktop PCs, laptops are also useful for communications in various different ways including:

- with other laptops and desktops in order to share files
- with a range of devices such as mobile phones and music players, again to share files
- with individuals and organisations via the Internet.

Mobile working is open to you if you have a laptop, and by this we mean both working as part of your paid job and working on whatever personal projects you may have on the go at any time.

You may well find that you use a range of different communications technologies for mobile working. What you will use is likely to vary depending on the task at hand.

In this chapter we look at the different methods of communication available to you, and what you might do with them.

What you'll do

PAN, LAN, WAN

The communications technologies: Ethernet

The communications technologies: Wi-Fi

Bluetooth

Infra red

3G and HSDPA

PAN, LAN, WAN ▶

We are going to encounter a lot of specialist terminology in this chapter, and to start off we are going to throw three definitions at you which should help to put everything we cover into a broader context.

PAN: Personal Area Network

A Personal Area Network or PAN is one in which you exchange information directly with another device.

Types of uses

If you have a mobile device that you want to keep up to date with information, such as a mobile phone, smartphone or PDA which can store your diary, you can set up a PAN between it and your laptop so that when you connect the two they exchange data easily and usually automatically.

Types of devices involved

- Mobile phones
- Smartphones, PDAs and handheld computers
- Mobile music devices
- Digital cameras

Technologies used

- Bluetooth
- Infra red
- Wired USB connection

LAN: Local Area Network

A Local Area Network or LAN is one in which you connect two or more devices together in order that they can share information with each other.

Types of uses

You will use a LAN if you have more than one computer and you want them to be connected. You will also use a LAN if you have an Internet connection provided by a separate modem and your computers connect to that.

Types of devices involved

- Laptop computer(s)
- Desktop computer(s)
- Printer(s)
- Broadband (ADSL) modem

Technologies used

- Wi-Fi
- Ethernet

WAN: Wide Area Network

A Wide Area Network or WAN operates over a very wide distance, for example a whole country. Large companies set up WAN networks to connect geographically separated offices. The Internet can be described as the world's biggest WAN.

Types of uses

Within large businesses WANs are used to share computers and data. At home you use a WAN when you use the Internet.

Types of devices involved

- Laptop computer(s)
- Desktop computer(s)

Technologies used

- Technologies provided by telecommunications companies and within organisations

Jargon buster

ADSL: Asymmetric Digital Subscriber Line. The technology you use to connect to the Internet. You do this via a modem which is connected to your phone line and your computer. People often use the term broadband instead of ADSL.

For your information

4

The range of a WAN is theoretically unlimited.

The communications technologies: Ethernet

Ethernet is a wired type of connection between one device and another. It is typically used for networking more than one computer together and for connecting to ADSL modems for Internet access (some ADSL modems also use a USB connector type). Ethernet is increasingly being displaced by wireless links, most notably Wi-Fi (see below).

Ethernet connections exist at different speeds, but you do not need to concern yourself with this as even the slowest currently available will be suitable for your needs.

Ethernet connections require a specific port on your laptop and on the connecting device, be it another laptop, a desktop, an ADSL modem or another device. The port is known as an 'RJ-45 port' or an Ethernet port.

The good news is that every laptop should have an Ethernet port. It is a rare laptop indeed that lacks one. To connect two devices such as a modem and a computer, you should not need any additional software. It will be enough to connect the two by cable.

Internal modem

With the development of ADSL or broadband Internet the use of internal modems in laptops has decreased over the past few years. Nonetheless many laptops still have internal modems which you will see referred to on specification sheets as 56K and V90 modems. The connector type is known as 'RJ-11' or modem connector.

We would not suggest that a 56K modem should be on your 'must have' list of specifications, but it is handy to have one as a backup, and the chances are a laptop you choose will have one whether you intend to use it or not.

If your laptop does have an internal modem, and you normally use a broadband Internet connection and this connection fails for any reason, then the 56K modem is a handy fallback. You will notice a marked reduction in connection speed if you do need to use it, though. You will need to set up a 'dial-up' Internet connection in addition to your broadband one and be

You will see Ethernet connections described in different ways on laptop specification sheets. You might see any of the following: 10/100, 10/100 Mbps, 10/1000, 10/1000 Mbps or 'Gigabit' Ethernet.

in a position to connect the telephone line cable to the RJ-11 port, for which you may need a phone extension cable.

The communications technologies: Ethernet (cont.)

Make an Ethernet connection

Using Ethernet to connect to your modem is easy.

1 Take the Ethernet cable.

2 Plug one end into your modem/router. There are likely to be several Ethernet sockets and it does not matter which one you use, but make sure the plug is the right way up. If it feels as though you are forcing the plug into the socket, then stop and turn it round. The plug should slide into the socket comfortably.

3 Plug the other end into your laptop. There will be only one socket that it will fit into. If there is a modem connector this could look similar, but the plug won't fit. The Ethernet connector is usually marked by a picture of three computer monitors connected together.

4 Your laptop should make the connection automatically. Look at the bottom right corner of the screen in the Notification Area to see an icon that shows you are connected.

The communications technologies: Wi-Fi

Wi-Fi is the name given to a wireless communications standard widely used for wireless networking. The tasks it is most frequently used for are:

- connecting one computer to others to allow them to share files or hardware, or in office environments connecting to a central 'server' computer on a larger network
- connecting a computer to a broadband (ADSL) modem for Internet access
- getting onto the Internet when you are away from your home or office using a 'hotspot', a public access service which may be free or charged for.

Let's look at these in a little more detail and explore the circumstances in which they may be appropriate for you.

Wi-Fi networking

At some point your home may include more than one computer. When you get to this stage you may want to share some resources between them. For example, a printer may be physically attached to one computer, but the other may sometimes need to print from it. Alternatively, one computer may have some files on it that another computer wants to access, such as important household documents, music files or family photos. You could simply copy these files from one computer to another every time they are changed, but this is tedious and time-consuming, and could take up considerable amounts of hard drive space on more than one computer unnecessarily.

With a Wi-Fi network, you can designate folders and resources such as a printer on any computer as 'shared', and so provide 'remote' access to them.

When it comes to printer sharing there are several options to choose from. Physically moving the printer from one computer to another, or taking the computer to the printer, are both possible but over time can become unpopular options, particularly if a lot of printing is required. Designating the printer as shared over Wi-Fi could be the ideal option.

Wi-Fi Internet access

There are two ways to connect computers to the ADSL router and modem which actually makes your Internet connection. You could use an Ethernet cable. Most ADSL router modems have four inputs for Ethernet, so you could connect four laptops with Ethernet cables. Your only additional expense is the cables themselves.

Ethernet capability is built into laptops, but if you want to connect a PC in this way you may also need to add Ethernet capability to it, so you would incur some added expense and would need to spend a little time configuring this for your desktop.

The upside of using Ethernet for this job is that it is very reliable, but the downsides are that you need to manage a fair amount of cabling around your home, and that you can only access the Internet where you have plugged an Ethernet cable into your computer. This could be something of an annoyance if one of your key reasons for buying a laptop is to allow you to be totally mobile within your home. And if you have a garden and have any aspirations to use the Internet from there, you can probably see an obvious constraint with Ethernet!

Wi-Fi as an alternative is appealing if you do not want trailing wires around your home. Your new laptop should have Wi-Fi built into it already. If you want to add a desktop into the mix you may need to add Wi-Fi to it. You can do this easily by buying a Wi-Fi USB adaptor. These are inexpensive and easy to fit – you don't need to do much more than plug them into a USB socket and install the software that comes with them.

Timesaver tip

Wi-Fi has a limited range. You will see product boxes that claim a range of up to 100 metres, but the actual range you achieve in your particular circumstances will vary depending on factors like the number of walls between one Wi-Fi 'access point' and another. This means you are unlikely to get a full 100 metres between your ADSL router and your laptop. Range and data speed may both be affected by distance, intervening features like walls, ceilings and the presence of other networks that are nearby.

The communications technologies: Wi-Fi (cont.)

Important

When using Wi-Fi to share access to computer files or to the Internet via an ADSL router and modem you need to be sure that your network has appropriate security settings. Without these your near neighbours or even people passing by in the street will be able to use your Internet access or access your files. For more on security and Wi-Fi see Chapter 9.

4

For your information

Power-line adaptors let you use your wall power sockets for Internet and network connection.

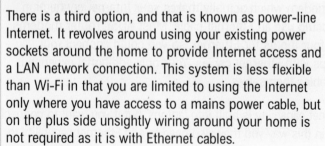

Timesaver tip

There is a third option, and that is known as power-line Internet. It revolves around using your existing power sockets around the home to provide Internet access and a LAN network connection. This system is less flexible than Wi-Fi in that you are limited to using the Internet only where you have access to a mains power cable, but on the plus side unsightly wiring around your home is not required as it is with Ethernet cables.

For your information

Wired versus wireless

When deciding what kind of network you want to install, you may want to weigh up the pros and cons of the two most common approaches of wireless (Wi-Fi) and wired (Ethernet). Each has its good and less good points. The trick is to find which system you think is likely to work best for you.

Wired (Ethernet)

- *Reliability*. You are not likely to experience interference from other nearby systems.

- *Maintenance*. Wired networks are generally easier to maintain than wireless ones as troubleshooting problems can be less complex.

- *Security*. A wired network is perfectly secure as only those who are physically plugged in can access the network.

- *Speed*. Wired networking can be a lot faster than wireless networking. This means you can exchange more information between computers more quickly, though for most uses a wireless connection is likely to be fast enough.

- *Planning*. You will need to work out where to put the wiring and how to fix it securely around your home. Trailing wires are a health and safety no-no as you or others can trip on them.

- *Location*. You are restricted to the access points you provide. Even in a single room this means you are unlikely to be able to move from one location to another very easily.

Wireless (Wi-Fi)

- *Portable*. You can use your laptop anywhere that is in range of your wireless network, such as in rooms of your home which do not have telephone lines or any permanent computer equipment, or even your garden.

- *Cost efficient*. If you are likely to want to use the Internet in lots of different places, then the price of setting up a wired (Ethernet) system could be higher than setting up a wireless (Wi-Fi) one.

- *Tidy*. With no wires to carry the signal between computer and modem you are able to be in a wire-free environment, which can be a lot tidier than one which relies on cables and is easier to manage.

- *Flexible*. When you want to use a new location for wireless access you simply need to make sure it is in your current wireless range. There is no need to set up a new set of wiring to the new location.

- *Complexity*. Some people can find it a little complex when they first set up a wireless network. The trick is to read the manuals that come with your equipment and make sure you understand the various aspects of the system.

- *Security*. You need to set up systems to ensure your network is safe and secure. This requires a little effort, but again the manual that comes with your equipment should walk you through the process.

- *Interference*. You may find that you need to take steps to eliminate interference from another nearby network in order to get the fastest speed from your network. Again the manual will help here.

The communications technologies: Wi-Fi (cont.)

Making a choice

Choose a wireless network if you:

- need access in lots of places around your home
- do *not* want wires around the home
- are confident you can set up a secure system.

Choose a wired network if you:

- only need access in one or two places in your home
- want the super fast speeds a wired network can offer
- are confident about doing the wiring safely.

Wi-Fi mobile Internet access

When you are out and about and want to access the Internet, for example to email or check something on the Web, you may be able to find a wireless 'hotspot'. These are often found in coffee shops, in railway stations and in other publicly accessible spaces. Some of these are free and others are charged for. Explore your local area to find out what is available.

Timesaver tip

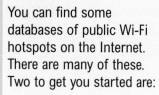

You can find some databases of public Wi-Fi hotspots on the Internet. There are many of these. Two to get you started are:

- the Wi-Fi Zone Finder at *http://wi-fi.jiwire.com/*
- Total Hotspots at *http://www.totalhotspots.com/*

To find more like this use a search engine such as Google (*www.google.co.uk*) and type in a search term, for example 'free public Wi-Fi in Manchester' or 'public hotspot finder'.

Connect to a wireless network

1. If you have got a wireless network at home connecting is easy. For example, in Windows 7 first make sure your router/modem is switched on.

2. Put the cursor over the network icon in the group in the Notification Area at the bottom right of the screen. It will say 'Not connected – Connections are available'.

3. Click the icon and you will be offered a list of available connections. There will probably be lots of modems/routers listed as the laptop will find all that are within range. Click the name of your router/modem and then click Connect.

4. If the modem/router is not password protected there will be a warning but you can choose to connect anyway by clicking Connect. If you have set up a password (which you should do, see Chapter 9) you will be asked to enter it. You'll only need to do this once.

5. Check the Notification Area for an icon that shows you are connected.

The communications technologies: Wi-Fi (cont.)

Wi-Fi standards

Before we move on from Wi-Fi we should spend a little time looking at the various Wi-Fi standards which exist.

When you look at laptop specifications you may see a range of labels applied to the Wi-Fi specification, all starting 802.11 and ending with a letter. You may also see the term 'Draft-N'. What do all these mean? As far as the average user is concerned the different names below relate primarily to data speeds.

802.11b, 802.11g	These two standards are entirely compatible with each other and can operate together on the same network. So if you have an older laptop with 802.11b built in and add a newer one with 802.11g, they will work together.
	The maximum theoretical data speed of 802.11b is 11 Mbps, while for 802.11g it is 54 Mbps.
	The 'g' standard is faster than the 'b' standard, and if you have a 'b' standard device on your network it will pull down the data speed of the 'g' devices to meet it.
802.11a	The 802.11a standard functions at the same speed as 802.11g, but it operates at a different radio frequency to 'b' and 'g'. This means it is not compatible with them.
	The 'a' standard is most often found in offices and very rarely anywhere else – such as in the home.
	That noted, you may well find that a laptop you like the look of is compatible with the 'a' standard. As long as it is also compatible with the standard you are using with other elements of your own network, for example other computers or your ADSL modem, then compatibility with the 'a' standard will not cause any problems for you.
802.11n	802.11n is a newer standard capable in theory of a maximum data speed of 100 Mbps. It functions on the same radio frequencies as the 'a', 'b' and 'g' standards and so is compatible with all of these, though you will only stand a chance of approaching the fastest data speeds if it is in an 'n' only environment. For a long time this standard was referred to as 'Draft-N'.

Bluetooth is a wireless technology designed typically to connect just two devices together for a short period of time, as a PAN or Personal Area Network. It is ratified by an organisation called the Bluetooth Special Interest Group, and is a universal standard. This means that devices should be able to communicate with each other regardless of their manufacturer.

Bluetooth has existed for some while and the standard has developed over time. You might encounter Bluetooth 1.0, 1.1, 1.2, 2.0 and 2.1.

All the different standards support different data speeds and features but they are all 'backwards compatible'. This means that a device with any of the standards should communicate with a device with any other standard.

Bluetooth is capable of a range of different functions, each one governed by a 'profile'. For a function to work the profile required needs to be on both the devices which are communicating with each other.

Different profiles cater for things like:

- wireless voice communication between a phone and a handsfree Bluetooth headset

- wireless communication with a device such as a mouse, keyboard or printer

- transfer of files between devices

- sharing of calendar, contacts and to-do information between devices (such as synchronising a mobile phone)

- sending stereo sound to headphones.

Bluetooth

Make a Bluetooth connection

1 Make sure Bluetooth is turned on and visible on the device you want to connect, for example your mobile phone.

2 Make sure Bluetooth is turned on, on your laptop. If there is a physical switch make sure it is in the on position.

4

For your information

Bluetooth is built into most modern laptops. However, if you buy a second-hand laptop it may not have Bluetooth built in. You can easily add it via an adaptor: there are many to choose from.

Bluetooth (cont.)

3 Find the Bluetooth application. For example, in Windows 7 click the arrow by the Notification Area at the bottom right of the screen to show hidden icons and then click the Bluetooth icon.

4 Choose Add a Device and wait while a window opens and displays available devices.

5 Double-click your device and then look at the device you are connecting to. If it asks for permission to add the laptop to its device list say yes.

6 Windows 7 will have presented a code which you need to enter onto your other device. Then you can wait while the connection is made. Your laptop may want to add some drivers which it gets from the other device, and you may need to give some permissions on the other device so keep checking both until the connection is complete.

7 When the connection is complete your new device will show up in the Devices and Printers section of your laptop. To see it click Start and choose Devices and Printers.

Infra red is regarded by many as an old technology and not worthy of great consideration. It is found in some but not all laptops, and a few but not all mobile phones, smartphones and PDAs.

Infra red has the advantage of being very easy to use to send files between one device and the next – you simply 'beam' them without needing to make a formal connection between devices. Its range is limited, and it requires a 'line of sight' or direct, unbroken connection between two devices. It is also rather slow.

Infra red is considered by many to have been overtaken by Bluetooth, but if your laptop and another device both have it present, you could find it useful for an easy, no-frills exchange of files on a one-by-one basis.

Infra red

4

3G and HSDPA

3G is a fast data communications technology provided by mobile network operators. It is often referred to as 'mobile broadband'. 3G is most frequently associated with mobile phones. Such phones are good for fast mobile Web access, data exchange such as uploading photos to websites and mobile blogging, speedy download of mobile email and, importantly, two-way video calling.

Jargon buster

HSDPA: High Speed Downlink Packet Access. A data download technology used by 3G mobile phone networks. Currently top download speeds available are 7.2 Mbps in a very few areas and 3.6 Mbps more widely. In the future connection speeds are expected to rise to 14.4 Mbps and network operator Vodafone has recently announced upgrade plans to accommodate this speed. Data connection speeds depend on services provided by your network operator.

Blog: a website you can produce to gather together your thoughts on a particular topic. Some people refer to blogs as online diaries, but they can be much more than this, covering anything from hobbies to political campaigns.

While most frequently associated with mobile phones, 3G and HSDPA 'mobile broadband' is also becoming more common in laptop computers. You can get mobile broadband in one of two ways:

- A built-in SIM card slot. This is most often found in business focused laptops at present. The SIM card fits into a slot on the laptop itself so that it is unobtrusive and can be left in place all the time.

- An add-on often referred to as a 'dongle' which slots into a USB port on your laptop. These are small – not much larger than a USB keydrive – though they do need to be large enough to accommodate a SIM card.

Mobile broadband in laptops was initially aimed primarily at business focused users but has now begun to make its way

For your information

The UK network operator websites are as follows:

3	*www.three.co.uk*
O2	*www.o2.co.uk*
Orange	*www.orange.co.uk*
T-Mobile	*www.t-mobile. co.uk*
Vodafone	*www.vodafone. co.uk*

into more consumer or home-user friendly laptops. It is becoming more common particularly in the small format, low-cost laptops known as netbooks.

Data communications speeds are the same as those available to mobile phone users: 3G speeds can theoretically achieve download speeds of 384 Kbps; HSDPA currently tops out at 3.6 Mbps though in some cases connections of 7.2 Mbps are available. In the future connection speeds are expected to become even faster.

If this is of interest then check network operator websites for the very latest information. When comparing the pricing of the services, make sure you also check on their coverage as data speeds can vary across different parts of the UK.

4

For your information

Mobile broadband lets you use the Internet at fast speeds from any location you can get a mobile phone signal. You'll need a 'dongle' that fits into a USB port and a contract from a network operator.

Looking after and upgrading your laptop

5

Introduction

When purchasing any computer it is important to think about your current and future needs if you want to get the best value from your acquisition. Just as when making any purchase, buying a computer to meet your current requirements without taking into account future needs may mean that you need to upgrade or change it fairly quickly.

This is more important where laptops are concerned than it is if you were choosing a desktop. This is because it is a lot easier to upgrade desktops in all kinds of ways. In fact, there is only a small range of upgrades you can make to a laptop yourself.

Given that laptops and desktops run the same operating systems you might find this to be a bit surprising. But the difference is not to do with the operating system itself. It is to do with the way the components in desktops and laptops are put together. Laptops tend to have a more integrated design, and their components are housed in a smaller casing than desktops, so there is little scope for changing elements of their internal make-up.

Desktop vs. laptop

Desktops are generally built inside fairly large cases. There is a main circuit board (or motherboard), which contains the processor and other key components.

Many components, such as graphics and audio management, are provided by separate circuit boards, which are plugged into the main board. When you order a desktop PC you can often choose between various options. Upgrading to a newer standard at a later date is a task many computer owners are prepared to take on themselves as it is usually only a matter of buying a new card, fitting it and installing any provided software.

Other components in a desktop PC, such as the hard disk, optical disks and flash card readers, are also fitted to the motherboard as separate items. They connect by wires, which allow them to sit in their bays in a desktop PC case, well away from the motherboard.

Still more components, most notably RAM memory, fit directly to the motherboard, and adding more is just a case of buying the right type and amount and slotting them into place.

Where laptops are concerned, upgrade options are rather more limited because of the way the components are fitted together.

It is possible to add components such as a second hard drive to a laptop, but this is usually achieved using either a 'modular bay' or a 'slab'. In both cases the additions involve using components which are external to your laptop and plug into it rather than opening it up and adding new components internally.

Did you know?

You can often choose your preferences when you buy a desktop PC, and it is not too difficult to make upgrades yourself at a later stage, for example adding a second hard drive.

Important

Laptops necessarily exist inside a small casing, which have very little spare and unused space inside them. They do not lend themselves to being opened up for having new components added.

Important

Modular bays or 'slabs' can't be used unless your laptop has been designed to accommodate them. Check the manufacturer's information before you buy a new laptop to see what is specifically available for it.

Timesaver tip

Any extra devices you buy, such as a slab or extra hardware to use in a modular bay, will add to your overall expenditure. Make sure you can afford what you want and that there isn't a less expensive way of getting it, such as buying a laptop which comes with two batteries.

A 'modular bay' is a slot in one side of your laptop. It may house an optical drive when you buy the laptop, but other optional components could be a second hard drive, a spare battery or even simply a 'space saver' – an empty cassette designed to block up the bay and make the laptop lighter to carry.

A 'slab' or expansion base is a section that fits to the underside of the laptop and can house an extra battery, optical drive or other components.

Did you know?

Some laptops can be expanded with extra batteries or extra ports and connectors using a separate base section.

For your information

The components that go together to make a laptop have often been chosen with their compatibility and collective performance in mind, to give you the best performance for the financial outlay you make.

5

Don't plan to upgrade

The best advice, on the basis of what you've just read, is never to buy a laptop with the thought in the back of your mind that you will upgrade it. It is better to buy a laptop that you feel will last you for the longest time possible, and when it reaches the end of its usefulness, to replace it with another.

If this sounds harsh, then note that we are not suggesting that laptops are a short-term, throwaway item. A well chosen laptop should give good service for up to five years if it is well looked after, and notwithstanding the kinds of unfortunate breakdowns that can affect all kinds of equipment.

By the same token, it is very important to take good care of your laptop, both inside and out. We will cover software related matters in Chapter 6 and security in Chapters 9 and 10, but later in this chapter we will look at how to keep the hardware itself spick and span.

By far the easiest internal upgrade you can make to a laptop is to add more RAM memory. Indeed, in many cases, it is the only internal upgrade you can make to a laptop.

RAM memory is a vital component of any computer. It provides the space a computer needs to store data it is currently using. The most obvious types of data are the applications which are running at any one time, and the information they contain.

For example, when you run a word processing application it is stored in RAM. As you type a document, that is stored in RAM too. Only when you save the document, or it is automatically saved by the software, does it get written to the hard disk and even then, if you are still working on it, your current working copy is stored in RAM.

All the time data is in RAM it is not saved anywhere safe. If your computer is inadvertently switched off for any reason, the content of the RAM memory will be lost. Much software often automatically tries to avert any problems by automatically saving what is in RAM at intervals, so that if your computer crashes you can recover what you were working on up to the last automatic save. However, this recovery is not guaranteed.

If you look at any software application, from an operating system to a word processor or a game, they will specify a minimum amount of RAM needed to run. If your computer has less than this amount, the software will struggle or may not run at all.

Upgrading RAM

Timesaver tip

If you can afford more RAM at the time of purchase, then it is probably the best upgrade to choose, not only because it can be cheaper to add at the time of purchase than later, but also because you save yourself the hassle of performing an upgrade later.

5

For your information

A useful source of advice and information is the website *www.crucial.com/uk*. This is the website of a memory seller, and it can perform an online scan of your laptop to help you identify the RAM memory it needs, or you can simply look up your laptop on the website.

Upgrading RAM (cont.)

Find out how much RAM your Windows 7 computer has

1. Click Start then click Control Panel.

2. Choose System and Security.

3. On the next screen under the System heading choose View amount of RAM and processor speed.

4. Look at the next screen which gives lots of information about the system specifications of your laptop. One of the bits of information provided is the amount of RAM installed.

The process

If you do find yourself needing to upgrade RAM the first task is to find out how much RAM your laptop has at the moment. If you aren't certain of the amount, your original invoice or other documents received at the point of purchase should specify this or you can find out on the laptop itself.

Next check the user manual for your laptop. This may tell you any of the following:

- how much RAM the laptop has
- the maximum amount the laptop can accommodate
- what capacities of RAM modules you need to buy to add to the existing RAM
- how to physically install the RAM.

Your laptop may be packaged with a paper manual, or one on a CD-ROM, or have the manual on the hard drive, or any mix of these. If you don't have the manual, take a look at the manufacturer's website to see if it is available to download. If not, or if you are in any doubt at all about what RAM to buy or how to make the installation, contact your laptop manufacturer directly for this information. You need an answer to all four points above.

Actually fitting the RAM should be straightforward. First you should switch off your computer. Unplug it and remove the battery, just to be absolutely certain there is no power running through the machine.

Your laptop manual will point you towards a cover for the RAM memory. This will usually be on the underside of the casing. You simply remove the cover, and slot the new RAM into the available socket. Replace the cover when you are done and that is the job finished.

When you switch the laptop back on, your laptop will acknowledge the new RAM memory and should work as usual with no additional effort required from you.

Many laptops have optical drives – a CD-ROM or DVD drive. Some of these drives can play Blu-ray movie disks. Some are LightScribe compliant. LightScribe lets you put your own designs onto an optical disk, giving them a professional look. You need to buy specially compliant disks to take advantage.

The optical drive may be in a fixed position, or it may be removable and in a 'modular bay' as noted above.

If the drive is removable your laptop manufacturer may sell other items that can fit into the drive housing, for example an additional battery or a second hard drive. Buying one of these extras could prove to be useful if you want to extend your computer's storage capacity or battery life.

Some ultraportable laptops lack an optical drive because there simply isn't room in the casing for one. It may be possible to add one via a USB port. Check with your laptop manufacturer to be clear on the options.

You can't add an internal optical drive to a laptop as an upgrade unless via a modular bay.

Optical drives

For your information

More information about LightScribe is at *www.lightscribe.co.uk.*

5

Upgrading your hard drive

On some laptops the hard drive is easy to remove. This means you can upgrade the hard drive, for example substituting a higher capacity drive if yours becomes full or if it becomes faulty in some way.

But you can't simply swap the old drive for a new one. The hard drive contains all the information your computer needs to use when you switch it on, including the operating system, as well as any applications you have installed and all your data. You need a way of swapping this from one drive to the other. The way to accomplish the upgrade is to 'clone' your existing hard drive onto the new one. There are several ways to do this.

You could buy an upgrade kit which will include a way of connecting the new drive to your laptop (usually by a USB cable), and some software for transferring an exact copy of your existing hard drive to the new one, i.e. making the clone. You will get instructions with the kit for making the clone, and when this is done you should be able to insert the new hard drive and it will function as normal.

Alternatively, you could use specialist software which makes an exact copy of your hard drive onto a CD. It will use as many CDs as it needs to make the copy, simply asking for a new disk when the one it is working on is full. An example of software like this is Norton Ghost, but there are many others.

When you have made a copy of your hard drive, you can remove the old drive and insert the new one, then boot your laptop with a CD (which the software will make for you) and then reinstall the copy of your old hard drive onto the new one.

Upgrading a hard drive needs to be undertaken with care, as if you damage your original hard drive in any way you won't be able to access the data and software it contains. Always make a backup before attempting this procedure, and never start it unless you are confident about what you are doing.

If you would rather just add a second hard drive, for additional storage, then a 'modular bay' may be the most convenient method as this will mean the second hard drive is permanently fitted inside your laptop and is always with you. Note, though, that if you remove an optical drive to insert a second hard drive, obviously the optical drive will not be accessible any more.

Another option is to use an external hard drive. These generally attach to your computer via USB or firewire connectors. You have two options here. Portable hard drives tend to be smallish in size so they are easy to carry around, while you can also get larger external hard drives. The latter type are quite bulky and not ideal to carry around all the time, but they can offer much more storage space than portable hard drives and so are good for making backups (see Chapter 8), or for storing data that you don't need access to all the time.

For your information

This external hard drive is too large to carry around on a regular basis, but it can function as a second storage medium at your desk, or be used as a backup device.

◀ Adding a second hard drive

Use an external hard drive

1 Your external hard drive should connect by USB. Check the manual to find out the precise steps to follow in order to set it up.

2 Follow the instructions perfectly to ensure the set-up process is done correctly. You must allow any drivers and additional software to be installed in the right order and this will be made clear in the hard drive instructions.

3 When you have completed the initial set-up you will be able to connect and disconnect the external hard drive as you need to without making any further installations.

4 You can view the contents of an external hard drive in the same way as the hard drive inside your laptop. For example in Windows 7: click Start; choose Computer; double-click the external hard drive.

5

Batteries

Remove and replace the battery

1 If it is in use, close your laptop and turn it off.

2 Turn your laptop over so you can see its underside.

3 Your battery is probably located at the back edge of the casing. Look for two latches, one at each end.

4 Slide the latches so that they are in the opened position.

5 Push the battery so that it slides away from the outer casing.

6 To replace the battery carefully line up any guidelines on the edge of the battery and the sides of its slot on the laptop.

7 Gently push the battery into position. It should go into its final location with a gentle click. Do not force it – the fitting procedure should be smooth.

Your laptop will have come with a battery which gives a certain amount of working time away from mains power. Some laptops are supplied with two batteries in order to help you prolong working life away from mains power.

The manufacturer may well also sell second batteries, with either the same capacity as the one that came with your laptop, or a higher capacity. You may choose to purchase one of these as an upgrade when you buy your laptop, or could opt to buy one at a later stage.

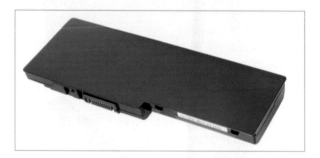

Fitting the battery is usually a simple matter, as the batteries in modern laptops tend to be easy to remove. Just look for the latch covers on the underside of the casing, remove one battery and replace it with the other.

Laptop batteries are not designed to last for ever. Eventually, no matter how well you care for it, your laptop battery will deteriorate and stop working altogether. You will notice degradation as the battery starts to run down more quickly over time. However, you can take steps to help your battery have the longest possible useful life:

- Don't allow your battery to fully discharge on a regular basis. A full discharge every now and again is, however, good for the battery.

- Store batteries in cooler rather than warmer places. It is likely that your battery will remain constantly in your laptop, so take care to store the whole thing in a cooler rather than a warmer place. If you have a second battery, some people even advocate storing it in a fridge when it is not in use. Don't put a battery in the freezer though!

- Having a second battery could be a good idea if you need to be able to work for prolonged periods away from mains power on a regular basis, but batteries start to deteriorate the minute they are manufactured. With that in mind it is not recommended you buy a second battery at the time of laptop purchase and store it in a cupboard unused as a long-term spare.

- If you do have two batteries for your laptop try to use them alternately so that both deteriorate at a similar rate. This should prevent you getting confused and using the more deteriorated one by accident when travelling. Store the spare battery in a cool place when it is not in use.

- Don't leave a battery fully discharged. Recharge it as soon as possible.

- Don't store a battery fully charged. It is better to store it at about 40 per cent charge.

- When you are using your laptop at a desk plugged into the mains it is a good idea to remove the battery. There is little point keeping the battery charging and with power flowing through it when it is not actually needed to keep your laptop working. The computer will function perfectly well without its battery plugged in if it is connected to the mains.

Did you know?

Some laptops come with a second battery for extra long life away from mains power.

Use software to help you prolong battery life

Your computer operating system has settings designed to help you prolong battery life. You will find a range of power schemes in the Control Panel in Windows which have pre-configured settings, and you can amend these to suit your own preferences if you wish.

You can make different settings depending on your current pattern of usage and whether your laptop is running on battery

5

Batteries (cont.)

or mains power. The settings have different names. Some are designed to give you longer battery life, some to maximise performance rather than battery life. You can configure as many different types of settings as you like and then switch between them as needed.

You may also find your laptop supplier has included some additional utilities to help conserve battery power. One option found on some laptops is an 'eco' button. This selectively turns off parts of the computer such as the optical drive and powered expansion slots, in order to save power after periods of time when they are not used.

How much power is left?

It is useful to know how much power is left in your battery at any one time. In Microsoft Windows, the easiest way to find out is to glance at the battery icon in the bottom right corner of your screen.

When the battery is charging you see an icon showing you that this is occurring. When the computer is running on battery power an icon shows you the amount of power left. If you want more information on this – including an estimate of how many minutes of computing time you have left – pass the cursor over the icon.

If you don't see any icon then it is not configured to display.

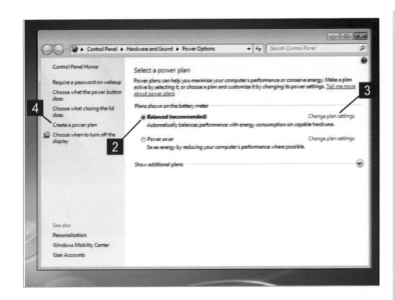

Check on battery power saving settings

1 To check on the power management settings of your battery right-click on the battery icon in the Notification Area and choose Power Options.

2 There will be various power plans available. You can choose the one which meets your requirements by making sure it is selected.

3 If you want to change any of the settings click Change plan settings. There are basic and advanced settings you can alter.

4 Alternatively you can create your own power plan by clicking Create a power plan.

5

Batteries (cont.)

Check on the status of your battery in Windows 7

1   Look at the Notification Area at the bottom right of the screen.

2   When you are charging your notebook pass the cursor over the battery icon in the Notification Area on the bottom right of the screen and a window will pop up telling you how much the battery is charged.

3   When the battery is not being charged passing the cursor over its icon will again tell you how much power remains.

Changing the settings

In Windows XP to change the setting go into the Control Panel and Power Options settings. You will find an option to show battery information in the Taskbar. Tick it and the icon will be displayed.

In Windows Vista to change the setting right-click anywhere on the Taskbar and choose Properties. Then click the Notification Area tab and make sure there is a tick by the Power system icon.

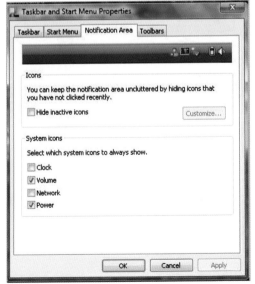

5

Batteries (cont.)

Make sure the battery charge status icon is displayed in the Notification Area of Windows 7

1. Put the cursor on the arrow in the Notification Area and click it to show hidden icons.

2. Choose Customise.

3. Click the drop down box next to the Power status information.

4. Choose one of the options by highlighting it then clicking.

5. Click OK.

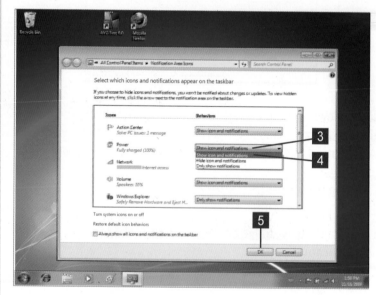

Going hand in hand with the issue of upgrading your laptop comes the one of caring for it on a day-to-day basis. Because a laptop is difficult to upgrade, it is important to look after the parts which can't be upgraded. Examples include the keyboard, screen and ports and connectors. So, let's look at some ways you can help protect your laptop day to day.

Laptop cases

If you transport your laptop from place to place frequently it is a good idea to have a protective case for it. At the most basic you could opt for a 'sleeve' type case. This is a slip style case that provides protection for your laptop but can't accommodate anything more such as power cables or papers.

There are many other types of cases which can accommodate more than just your laptop, including rucksacks, over the shoulder bags, flight cases and even cases you can use as bicycle panniers. Such laptop cases often have a separate section just for the laptop itself, other sections for papers, and still more sections for power adaptors and peripherals.

Using a case with a separate section for your laptop will help prevent cosmetic damage such as scratches to the casing, but can also help prevent damage to ports and connectors.

Timesaver tip

Some laptops have a clasp that connects the lid and bottom sections together, others do not. Without this clasp, if you carry a laptop in a bag without its own special section there is a possibility pens, paper clips and other objects could slip inside and damage the screen and/or keyboard. In such situations a sleeve type case, which will ensure the laptop remains closed, could be a good choice.

5

Taking good care of your laptop (cont.)

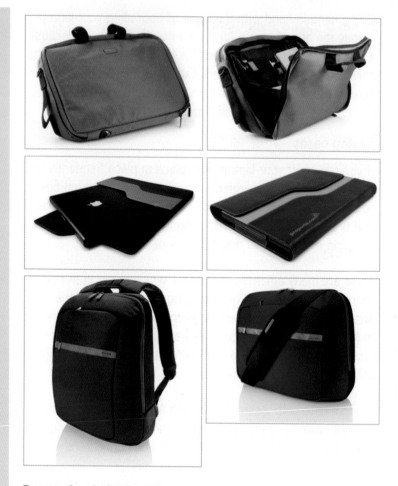

Prevention is better than cure

You can clean certain parts of your laptop at regular intervals (see later). It is also a good idea to be generally careful when you are using your laptop in order to keep it clean on an everyday basis and prevent serious disasters happening.

Do not drink near your laptop

It is easy to spill liquid onto your laptop. Do this and it can seep into the keyboard. There is electricity running through your laptop, and liquids and electricity are not a good mix. At the worst your laptop can be rendered unusable by liquids spilt onto it.

Do not eat near your laptop

Food crumbs can easily drop between the keys of your laptop, and can cause keys to stick or stop working. Other foodstuffs can create sticky messes on the keyboard which can make it uncomfortable to use.

Keep things tidy

When you have finished using your laptop remove any attached peripherals and put them away in order to protect them from being knocked onto the floor or otherwise damaged. Close the lid of your laptop and put it away in the drawer or cupboard where you store it. This will mean that you can't accidentally damage your laptop.

Do not put heavy weights on your laptop

If you leave your laptop on a table with its lid down, do not put anything onto it. The screen is made of several layers very close to each other and is very delicate. The lid is designed to protect the screen, but heavy objects could cause damage.

Lift by the base

If you want to lift or move your laptop around when it is opened do not pull at the screen or lift up the laptop by the screen. This could damage the hinges or affect the wiring which connects the upper and lower sections, causing severe damage to the screen. The ideal is to close your laptop lid before moving it around. If you must move it with the lid up, then hold it carefully by the base.

Open and close your laptop gently

The connection between lid and keyboard section of your laptop is very important. If it becomes damaged the screen may fail and your laptop can be rendered useless. Be careful when you

Dos and don'ts

Important

As soon as you get your new laptop make a note of the make and model and the serial number. Keep this in a safe place, such as where you keep other information for household insurance purposes.

Did you know?

Some laptops boast having a spillproof keyboard. This will provide some protection against liquids but it should not be relied upon.

5

open and close your laptop. Use smooth rather than jerky movements to open and close the lid, and when closing it do so slowly. Do not bang down the lid onto the keyboard section.

Do not rub the screen with abrasive materials

The screen of your laptop can be easily scratched. If you notice it is dusty or dirty do not rub at it with a sleeve in case buttons on the sleeve scratch the screen. Do not use abrasive household cloths on the screen. Only clean the screen with appropriate materials (see below for more on cleaning the screen).

Take care with the power cord

Do not tug the power cord out of its slot on your laptop sharply. Make sure you pull it out gently. Pull it out and push it in at a straight angle so as to avoid putting undue pressure on the connector. Do not wrap the cord tightly when preparing it for storage as this can damage the internal wires. Think carefully about where you put the power cable when it is plugged in. Make sure you are not likely to step on or trip over the cord if it trails off your desk towards the mains power socket. This could damage the cord, your laptop and yourself!

Use the correct ports

When plugging in peripherals make sure you use the right connectors. Your laptop is likely to have several different types of connector, and you may find, particularly at first as you familiarise yourself with your laptop and its peripherals, that you need to take care that you plug the right connector into the right slot. Forcing the connector into the wrong slot can cause irreparable damage both to the peripheral and to your laptop.

Keep your laptop flat when inserting peripherals

Do not tilt your laptop when inserting peripherals. If there is already a peripheral inserted on the opposite side, tilting your laptop to get at a slot can put stress on the slot already in use, and this can cause severe damage to the slot and to the peripheral connected to it.

Take special care of removable parts

If your laptop has a removable optical drive or other component, take very good care of it. Replacement parts are likely to be expensive. Store the component carefully, and if at all possible keep it in a protective box when not in use rather than loose in a drawer.

Do not force drives or other peripherals

If you use removable drives, flash memory cards, PC cards or other peripherals, be aware that you do not need to apply a great deal of pressure to get them into the required sockets. They should slot into place with a gentle click or simply push in. If you feel you are applying too much pressure, remove the peripheral and start again. Forcing a peripheral can cause damage both to it and to the slot it is intended for, and this damage could be irreparable.

Protect the fan

The processor in your laptop gets warm as it works. In order to keep it cool and prevent overheating some laptops have fans. Others dissipate heat throughout the casing without the need for a fan. They may still have grilles to allow hot air to escape easily. If your laptop has a fan or grilles take care that you don't block these with other equipment. Doing so can prevent heat dissipation and cause your laptop to overheat and be damaged.

5

Cleaning jobs

Clean your laptop screen

1. Turn off your laptop so that you have a good view of the screen.
2. Make sure the cloth you are going to use is clean.
3. Put a small amount of cleaning fluid on the cloth.
4. Gently wipe the screen with the cloth.
5. Check the cloth. If it is getting dirty, refold it and use another part of it to clean a new section of the screen with a fresh application of cleaning fluid.
6. Take care not to press hard on the screen, and do not use too much liquid at once.

It is advisable to clean your laptop at regular intervals. The precise intervals will vary depending on how often you use your laptop. What is important is that you decide on a regime and stick to it.

Clean the keyboard

Computer keyboards can harbour all kinds of dirt and germs. Dust and small particles of food and other materials can cause damage to the keyboard mechanics as well as being unhygienic, and so it is a good idea to try to keep your laptop keyboard as clean as possible.

There are varying degrees of laptop keyboard cleaning. At the most straightforward you can buy a keyboard vacuum. You should be able to find one for about £10. They can be powered from the USB port on your laptop so that they do not need any external power. They can be used to suck up crumbs and other small items that get lodged in between the keys. Some have attachments to help you get in between the keys. They may also have a brush attachment which can be used to clean ports and fan vents too.

There are more complicated cleaning methods which involve disassembling your keyboard, but these are not to be advised unless you are supremely confident. If you make a wrong move you can ruin the keyboard, and a laptop without a working keyboard is about as much use as a chocolate teapot.

Clean the screen

It is very easy for a computer screen to become dirty. It is second nature to touch it from time to time, pointing at things to show them to other people, for example. Computer screens can also attract dust and general grime. So cleaning the screen from time to time is important.

However, you need to take care when cleaning the screen. There are two elements to consider – the cleaning liquid and the cloth – and both need to be appropriate to the job in hand.

Choosing a cloth

It is not advisable to wipe a computer screen with an abrasive cloth as this can leave tiny scratches on it. Even a soft cloth can drag dust particles around the screen and cause scratching. You may also want to avoid using materials like tissues as these can leave tiny bits behind on the screen.

The ideal cloth is a soft cotton which is lint free or the kind of microfibre cloths that are used to clean spectacles.

The liquid

You can use tap water or distilled water. You can also use cleaner that is designed for spectacles. Be very cautious about using generic household cleaners as some may contain chemicals that are not screen friendly.

If you are concerned about a DIY solution, then you can buy a kit that comprises a liquid solution to put on the screen and wipes to clean the screen.

Timesaver tip

You may come across a keyboard cleaner in the form of a canister that blows air. These are not such a good idea and generally are to be avoided. This is because while it is possible to blow crumbs and other matter away from your keyboard, it is also possible to blow such items further into the keyboard where they become impossible to remove.

5

Cleaning jobs (cont.)

Timesaver tip

When cleaning the screen turn off the computer first. You will find it a lot easier to see the smears and grime you want to remove with the screen turned off, and will be able to tell when your screen is cleaned too.

Do not use a lot of liquid at a time. If liquid beads and drips down the screen it could get inside your laptop and cause considerable damage. If you are using a DIY solution moisten the cloth you are using rather than soaking it. A commercial cleaning kit should deliver a controlled amount of liquid direct to the screen via a pump action spray system.

You clearly need to apply some pressure when cleaning your screen but be careful not to apply too much. Laptop screens are made up of several delicate layers and if you apply too much pressure you could damage these.

Did you know?

You can buy special cleaning fluid for your laptop screen, such as the Proporta Mobile Device Cleaner.

Software matters

Introduction

Your computer will come with an operating system already installed. This will provide you with everything you need to get started, but the chances are that you will benefit from some additional software from the very earliest stages.

There are literally thousands of applications you can get hold of to boost your laptop's capabilities, and in some cases you will choose specialist software tools because you have specialist requirements.

However, many people will find that a basic selection of software added to what comes with their laptop will help them get the most from it from the start, only adding new software when they feel they need something more specialised for a particular task or set of tasks.

You can spend a lot of money on software – easily doubling what you spent on the laptop itself and almost certainly going way beyond that. But this is not necessary. There are many free applications available, and these can provide perfectly adequate software for general needs.

So in this chapter we look at the essential software add-ons for your new laptop, and we concentrate on what you can get for free.

What you'll do

Avoiding software overload

What you get at the start

The essential software extras

Computer security

Web browsing and Web utilities

Working with words and numbers

Diary and contacts management

Email

Music

Video

Photos

Backing up

Although there are many thousands of applications you can add to your laptop, you might want to progress slowly and steadily. Adding huge numbers of applications to your computer can result in having more software than you can use effectively. There are two key consequences:

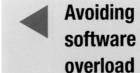
■ You can become confused by the amount of software you have installed. This is a possibility if you choose several applications that can do the same job, install them all, and then proceed to use different ones at different times. It is easy to become confused in this way.

■ You can cram your hard drive with software you are never likely to use. This not only takes up hard drive space but, if the software likes to run something in the background, such as an automatic checker for updates, it can clog up your computer's RAM memory (see Chapter 5) and make it run more slowly than it should.

Nevertheless, one of the key pleasures some people get from their laptop is trying out new software. Even if this idea does not appeal to you, if you have a particular task you want to achieve it can be a good idea to try several applications in order to find the one that suits you best.

So how do you avoid the two pitfalls mentioned above? The easiest way out of this dilemma is to use a method of testing software over a period of time and ensuring you delete what you do not intend to use. Fortunately this system should be inexpensive – free in fact.

It is very common for you to be able to download trial versions of software which will function for a few days before requesting that you register them by paying for them. Fail to pay and they will cease to function. This gives you an excellent opportunity to test and try software to find out if it does what you need it to do and if you get on with the way it works.

So there is nothing to stop you trying out software as much as you like – but don't forget to delete it if you decide not to use it in the long term.

What you get at the start

When you switch on your new laptop for the very first time it will already have some software installed. There are three possible sources for this software.

1 The operating system

The most significant part of your new computer in terms of software is its operating system. This will be pre-installed when you take your computer out of its box.

The operating system provides essential software that lets your computer work efficiently. We discussed operating systems in detail in Chapter 3.

As well as providing software necessary for your computer and the hardware associated with it to run smoothly, the operating system includes a number of utilities and applications which are considered by the operating system vendors to be part of the operating system rather than entirely separate applications.

2 Software from the computer manufacturer

In addition hardware manufacturers can add utilities and software to a computer which they have decided to provide free for your use. This can range from quick and easy ways to get to the system settings provided in the operating system through to multimedia viewers and other utilities.

3 Trial versions

Finally, software vendors can negotiate with hardware manufacturers to get trial versions of their software installed. These are often fully featured, time-limited trials. In the case of some kinds of software, such as anti-virus tools, they can come with several months of free subscription to automatic updates.

For your information

Applications which come to you in these three ways are not your only option and you do not have to use them. There are alternatives available in every case. Some are likely to do the same jobs in a way that is more to your liking.

However, be aware that in some cases you will be required to use particular software if you have particular hardware. For example, if you want to use an Apple iPod or iPhone you are required to have the Apple iTunes software. Even in this case you can use other software for actually managing your music.

As we have already noted there are literally thousands of applications you could consider adding to your laptop in order to boost its efficiency and help you do your computing more effectively.

We have chosen nine key areas in which we think you may want to consider using add-on software from the very earliest days of having your laptop. As you get more experienced, you are likely to find there are other categories you want to explore for yourself. We have chosen to look at the following:

- computer security
- Web browsing and Web utilities
- working with words and numbers (word processing, spreadsheets)
- diary and contacts management
- email
- music
- video
- photos
- backing up.

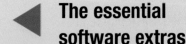

The essential software extras

6

Computer security

We look at computer security in greater detail in Chapters 8 and 9, so here we are just going to take a quick overview.

It is highly likely you intend to use the Internet with your computer. With this in mind the very first thing you need to think about is ensuring your computer's security from the first moment that you go online. There are several types of software you need for this purpose:

- anti-virus
- anti-spyware
- firewall.

Anti-virus software protects your computer against viruses which can infect your machine and do all kinds of damage, from deleting files you need to turning your computer into an email robot sending out emails without your knowledge or consent.

Anti-spyware software is designed to catch and delete a wide range of software that can do many different kinds of things. Examples of spyware include keyloggers which can be very malevolent. They can monitor your use of your keyboard and can pick up on passwords, credit card numbers and other personal information and send this out to someone else to use without your knowledge or consent.

Firewall software prevents unauthorised access to your computer. This could be either by computers a long way away from you which use the Internet to find unprotected computers and then plant software on them, or computers closer to home, such as those of people trying to get onto your wireless network and use the Internet for free.

What comes with your operating system?

If you run Windows 7, XP or Vista you will already have a firewall built in. There is anti-spyware software called Windows Defender which is built into Windows 7 and Vista, and which you can download for Windows XP.

Depending on who you bought your computer from there may also be trial versions of third party software included.

Some free alternatives

(For more information on this topic and more example software see Chapter 9.)

- AVG Anti Virus
  From: *http://free.avg.com*

- Avast! Antivirus
  From: *http://www.avast.com/*

- Zone Alarm firewall
  From: *http://www.zonealarm.com*

- Comodo
  From: *http://www.personalfirewall.comodo.com/*

- Ad-Aware
  From: *http://www.lavasoft.com*

- Spybot Search and Destroy
  From: *http://www.safer-networking.org*

- SpywareBlaster
  From: *http://www.javacoolsoftware.com*

Timesaver tip

It is generally not advisable to run more than one anti-virus utility, one anti-spyware utility and one firewall at a time. Running more can cause your computer to run slowly, and could cause other problems too.

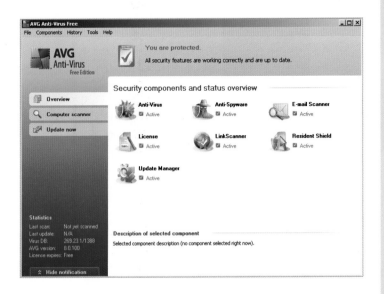

Computer
security (cont.)

Most people who get a computer spend a good deal of time using the Web. There are hundreds of thousands of websites covering every topic you could ever think of and there are sites that you will find useful for both leisure and work.

You may even find yourself wanting to become more involved in the Web and design your own website (or more than one if you get the bug!).

We can't possibly cover the whole scope of the Web here. Instead we will concentrate on listing just a few types of websites that might make a useful place to start your exploration of what is available.

Note, though, that even within the few categories we have selected, there are many, many more websites offering the services we list than we have space to mention here.

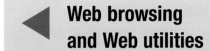

Web browsing and Web utilities

6

Requirement	Examples	Details
Photo sharing	Flikr *www.flickr.com* PhotoBucket *www.photobucket.com*	Photo sharing websites allow you to upload photographs in order to let others see them. Some online photo printing services also offer image sharing facilities.
Social networking	MySpace *www.myspace.com* Facebook *www.facebook.com* Bebo *www.bebo.com*	Social networking websites allow you to maintain online contact with your friends and share information about your activities and hobbies.
Blogging	Blogger *www.blogger.com* LiveJournal *www.livejournal.com* Wordpress *www.wordpress.com*	Blogging websites allow you to create your own online information store. Some people refer to blogs as online diaries, but they can be much more than this, covering anything from hobbies to political campaigns. Information is organised by date as well as by categories which you assign.
Video sharing	YouTube *www.youtube.com* MySpace Video *http://vids.myspace.com/* Google Video *http://video.google.com*	Video sharing websites allow you to upload your own videos and watch those others have made.

▶

Web browsing and Web utilities (cont.)

Requirement	Examples	Details
Shopping	Go to a search engine and look for your favourite high street stores. Also try price comparison to help you get the best deal online. Examples include: Pricerunner *www.pricerunner.co.uk* Kelkoo *www.kelkoo.co.uk*	Many high street stores have their own website and you can buy anything from books to groceries, clothes to holidays on the Web. If you have a specialist interest or hobby you may find online stores that can serve it more easily than the high street.
Catching up on missed TV	BBC iPlayer *http://www.bbc.co.uk/iplayer/* Channel 4 4oD *http://www.channel4.com/*	Increasingly popular in the UK is the ability to catch up on full versions of TV programmes you have missed. The BBC leads the way with the iPlayer, but others are following suit.
Travel	Streetmap *http://www.streetmap.co.uk* Multimap *http://www.multimap.com/* RAC route planner *http://route.rac.co.uk* The AA route planner *http://www.theaa.com/route-planner* Google maps route planner *http://maps.google.co.uk*	If you want to go somewhere these sites are good for getting driving directions. You can print them out for use away from the computer.

Did you know?

You can share digital photos with others using websites like Flickr, at *www.flickr.com*.

Did you know?

You can start writing a digital diary, also known as a blog, at sites like Blogger, at *www.blogger.com*.

Web browsing and Web utilities (cont.)

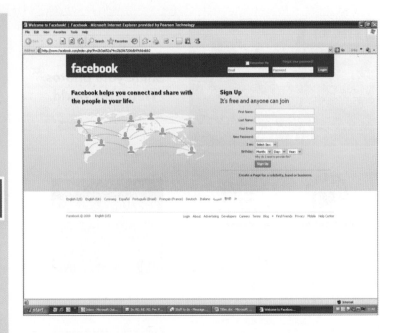

Did you know?

You can maintain virtual friendships and share files online at sites like Facebook, at *www.facebook.com*.

Searching the Internet

Because the Internet is so vast it is a good idea to familiarise yourself with ways of searching its contents and filtering the millions of websites which exist in order to get to the content you want.

There are many, many search engines which index Web content, and some have specialities. Here are just a couple you might like to try to get you started:

- Google *www.google.com*
- Yahoo *www.yahoo.com*
- Ask *www.ask.com*
- Technorati *www.technorati.com* specifically designed for searching blogs.

?

Did you know?

Google is the Internet's most popular search engine.

Signing up for websites

Some websites require you to sign up before you can fully use their services. For example, some shopping sites maintain an account which you can access via a password. This account can store billing information, delivery addresses (yours and others to which you send purchased goods, for example as birthday gifts) and information about items you've ordered, items you might like to order in the future, personal profile details and so on.

Other sites work on a membership basis. Facebook, mentioned above, is just one example of many. You simply can't get access to the services offered unless you sign up, at which point you become a member and can interact with others.

Web browsing and Web utilities (cont.)

Timesaver tip

- Don't sign up to websites if you are not confident about how they will treat your data. If you don't think they can keep your information securely, don't sign up.

- Read the 'privacy policy' on a website. If you don't like what you read, don't sign up.

- Look for checkboxes which let you opt into or out of receiving marketing information. A website may offer you the chance to opt in or out of receiving marketing information from it, and also from 'partner' organisations. If you choose to opt in you may get marketing emails or even post from a wide range of places that may or may not interest you.

This kind of system has benefits for you and the website owner.

For you:

- there is less work to do typing in information every time you visit a site

- you can maintain lists of things you are 'watching' or would like to purchase at some point

- you can set up preferences and maybe customise the way a website looks when you visit it

- you can maintain a list of delivery addresses for friends and relations, making it easier to buy gifts and get them sent on without having to type their addresses every time.

For the website owner:

- the site can develop an ongoing relationship with you if it knows your history so that it can make recommendations to you on the basis of previous activity

- the site can send you regular emails if you allow this, alerting you to new offers or services

- the site can get an understanding of the usage patterns of its members, which might help it develop new services that meet emerging requirements.

When this system works it can be mutually beneficial and work very well indeed. But things can go wrong. When you sign up with a website you may divulge your name and address. If you also buy from the website you are likely to need to part with your credit card information too. Websites can be broken into and details of their members stolen. This could lead to identity fraud problems.

With that in mind you should always take care when you sign up at websites.

Some free Web browsing software

- Firefox *www.firefox.com*
  Firefox is an increasingly popular alternative to Web browsers provided with your operating system. It can be customised in lots of different ways. Once you have obtained the basic Web browser you can extend its functions by choosing from hundreds of plug-ins, thereby customising it to suit your own requirements.

- Opera *www.opera.com*
  Opera is another free Web browser that comes in versions for mobile devices as well as for PCs. It claims to be faster than Internet Explorer and Firefox on the PC.

- Safari for Windows *www.apple.com/safari*
  Released in 2008 for Windows one of the draws of Safari is that it claims to be a lot faster at downloading Web pages than Internet Explorer, Firefox and Opera.

Each of these browsers has a range of features beyond simply opening Web pages. It is worth visiting their websites to find out what they might be able to offer you. Even when you choose one browser over another you might want to check rival browser websites from time to time as new versions appear and new features are added.

However bookmarks (records of websites you like and will want to visit again) are not automatically transferable between different browsers. You can transfer them between browsers manually as they all have import and export functions. There are also many websites where you can store bookmarks online so you can access them from any computer. Some even synchronise bookmarks between one computer and another. An example is Xmarks (*www.xmarks.com*). But a more efficient idea, particularly for a newcomer to laptop computing, is to choose a single browser and stick with it.

Timesaver tip

Having more than one Web browser installed on your computer will not render any other Web browser you have installed inoperable. You can use more than one browser at the same time with no problems at all.

Working with words and numbers

Whatever else you do with your computer you are likely to spend a fair amount of time working with words and numbers. A good word processor and spreadsheet can be the most important software add-on for many computer owners. There are many kinds of activity you can undertake with these.

Examples of work with words:

- writing letters of which you need to keep copies for your own reference
- writing longer documents such as reports
- creative writing
- producing leaflets, newsletters or magazines for a local club or society.

Examples of work with numbers:

- keeping track of your personal finances including things like household budgeting, savings plans for a specific goal such as a holiday, or managing your savings and investments
- managing the finances for a club or society you are involved with
- counting or adding activities of many kinds, for example keeping a tally of your time and distances if you are doing any kind of sports or keep fit activity.

Online alternatives

An interesting growth area over the last year or so has been the development of online word processors and spreadsheets. These have some advantages and some disadvantages.

Advantages:

- You can access your working documents from anywhere that you can get onto the Internet, and from any computer.
- Nothing is stored on your computer so if it is lost or stolen your documents remain accessible to you and safe from prying eyes.
- You can share documents which are being worked on easily with other people.

Disadvantages:

- You may not be able to carry documents with you as they are not stored locally on your computer.
- If for any reason you don't have access to the Internet, then you don't have access to your documents.

This last disadvantage can be overcome if you are able to download documents from your Web store onto your laptop for local editing.

What comes with your operating system?

Windows XP, 7 and Vista come with two applications, NotePad and WordPad. They both allow you to make text-based notes, and the latter is a simple word processor you can use to create documents complete with different fonts, font sizes and colours. But they lack some features which you might expect from a modern word processor, such as automatic checking of spelling and grammar.

What's free?

There are some free alternatives:

- For use on your computer there is OpenOffice.org (*www.OpenOffice.org*). OpenOffice is a free suite of software for word processing, spreadsheets, presentations, graphics and database management.
- For use online there is Zoho (*www.zoho.com*). Zoho includes a large range of utilities including word processing, spreadsheet, presentations, Web conferencing, diary planning, project management and more.
- Google Docs (*http://docs.google.com*) also lets you create documents, spreadsheets and presentations online. You can share these with other people.

Working with words and numbers (cont.)

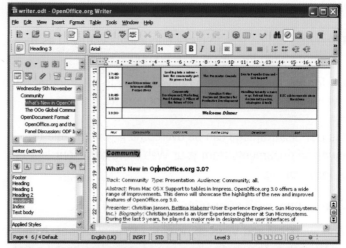

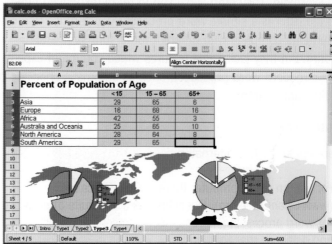

Use the built-in word processor in Windows 7

1 Click Start then hover the cursor over All Programs and a list will appear from which you can choose Accessories.

2 Click WordPad and the WordPad word processor will open and you can start typing.

3 Use the Font formatting tools to change the size, font, style and colour of your text.

4 Use the Paragraph tools to insert bulleted lists, align the text left, right or centre on the screen, insert indented text or change the line spacing.

5 Use the Insert tools to add pictures, drawings made with the Windows Paint software or other things into your document.

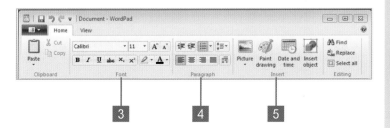

Working with words and numbers (cont.)

6 When you are done click the top right menu, choose Save As and choose a file format. A good format if you want to import the text into other word processing software is Rich Text.

7 Give your document a name then choose Save.

8 If you want to save it in a specific folder, select this from the list on the left before saving.

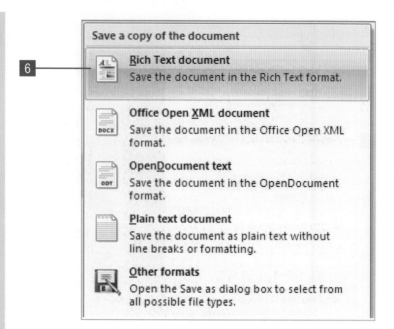

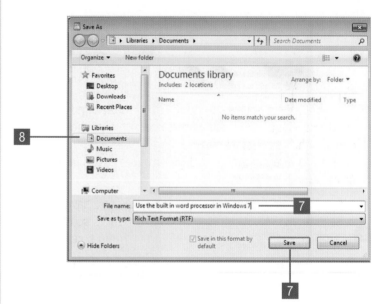

Most of us have fairly complicated diaries involving commitments for work, family life and leisure time. Keeping track of everything on both a day-to-day basis and looking further into the future can be tricky.

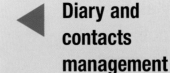
For many people the solution is a paper diary, but it is easy for this to become confused, with changed entries over time, things being crossed out and moved to other dates. A diary kept on your computer can be a lot 'cleaner'. It also has some other advantages over paper. For example:

■ You can set up 'recurring appointments'. These are useful for both work and home life. For example, if you have certain home related tasks you do on a regular basis – once a month, once a quarter and so on – you can schedule them as a 'recurring' diary task, entering them once and then having them repeat automatically at intervals you specify.

■ You can get good 'at a glance' views of things. If, for example, you are able to tag holidays, birthdays and other types of commitment, you may be able to display them all in a single view covering the year ahead, a selection of months ahead, and so on.

■ Diaries are great for keeping track of birthdays and other anniversaries. Enter an anniversary or birthday once and you can ask the calendar software to repeat it every year, even giving you a reminder a few days or a few weeks in advance of the event.

■ It is easy to find diary entries. If you know you have a scheduled event but can't remember when it is scheduled for, it is easy to search just by typing text into a search bar.

■ Computer diaries also often manage 'to-do lists'. These are lists of things that you want to do, but that can't be fitted into a specific time slot in the diary.

■ If you have a paper diary and lose it, you lose all your information in one fell swoop. If it is stored on a computer and you lose this, you should have a backup so that you can get to your information again quickly.

Computerised diaries can often also manage contacts, and again having your contacts stored on a computer has some serious advantages over using a paper address book.

Diary and contacts management (cont.)

Synchronising your laptop with a mobile device

1. Check the manual of the device you want to synchronise with.

2. If it runs Windows Mobile you can use the Sync Centre which is already installed in Windows 7.

3. If it runs another operating system there may be software on a CD that came with the device, or you may be advised to download software from the Web.

4. Whatever option is chosen you may be able to synchronise calendar, diary and to-do list information, back up the mobile device onto your laptop, and copy files such as pictures and music from the device to your laptop. Check the manual for the full details on how to do these tasks.

For example:

- You can search for contacts quickly and easily by name, or by any other information.

- You can print address lists or address labels made up from different groupings of contacts.

- If you store email addresses with your contacts you can simply click on the email addresses in order to send an email.

- You can group contacts together and if you use your contact software for email too you can easily send one email to all the members of the group.

- If you keep your contacts in a paper address book and lose it, you will lose everything and will need to rebuild your address book from scratch. If it is stored on a computer you should have a backup and so you will be able to get to your information quickly.

Synchronising with other devices

One further advantage of keeping your diary and contacts on your computer is that you can 'synchronise' this information with other devices.

So, for example, if you have a mobile phone, smartphone or a PDA or handheld computer of any kind, it may be possible to connect it to your computer and then share diary and contact information with it. This will give you a copy of your diary and contacts to carry around in your pocket, while another copy remains safely on your computer.

With this information on a mobile device you may be able to make changes to diary and contacts information while you are on the move, adding a new contact, changing details for existing contacts, adding new appointments or editing existing ones. When you get back to your computer and synchronise the information your laptop will reflect the changes you have made.

What comes with your operating system?

Windows 7 does not have a built-in calendar application. Windows Vista comes with Windows Calendar which allows you to manage your diary. Windows XP also has a built-in calendar application.

What's free?

There are some free alternatives for use online:

- Google Calendar (*http://calendar.google.com*).
  An online calendar that includes standard features like automated reminders for events allowing different people to add events – so that family, friends or work colleagues can produce a shared schedule.

- Yahoo! calendar (*http://calendar.yahoo.co.uk*).
  An online calendar with day, week and month views, this is linked to your Yahoo email and contacts stores.

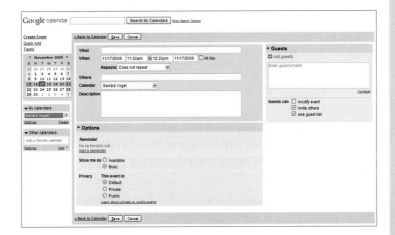

?

Did you know?

Just as with word processors and spreadsheets there are online diary and contact managers. You can share these with other people, making them a useful resource if you need to coordinate your time with other people who aren't always physically nearby.

Email

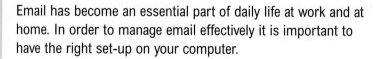

Email has become an essential part of daily life at work and at home. In order to manage email effectively it is important to have the right set-up on your computer.

Some people manage their email entirely using the online services of their Internet Service Provider (ISP), accessing email through their Web browser. Check what your ISP offers. There should be a page on its website where you can log in using a password, and then see all the email that has been sent to you, compose replies and so on.

There may be files and folders for organising email, and an online address book for you to keep details of your contacts readily to hand. This kind of system lets you manage your email without needing to have any software at all for the purpose on your computer. If you are sent an attachment you want to keep you can download it to your computer easily.

Some people like doing their email like this because it means they can access it from any computer that can get onto the Internet, providing they have their password to hand.

There are some disadvantages to doing email in this way and two in particular are worth considering.

When you are not connected to the Internet you can't access your email. So you can't check on what somebody has sent to you, or compose emails, until you go online. This may not be too important if your computer is always logged onto the Internet, but when you are away from home, you may find it more difficult to get online.

You are likely to have more than one email address. Your ISP will give you one, but you may also get a free one from a service such as Yahoo (*www.yahoo.co.uk*) or Google (*www.google.com*). Some people like to use different email addresses for different purposes, and you may find you fall into this camp after you have been using email for a little while.

To save you from checking several online email accounts you could choose to forward email from all your separate accounts to one main account. This would allow you to use just one 'Webmail' location to check all your email accounts.

To find out if this is possible with any of the email accounts you have, log on to them and take a look at the preferences or settings area.

The alternative to doing your email online is to use software on your computer that is designed to manage email. This can download messages and attachments from many different addresses in one sweep, and then store them in a single 'inbox' so that you can see all your emails at once and go through them at your leisure. Attachments are automatically filed away on your computer, and you can move them to the place that suits you best if you want to keep them in the longer term.

Email software on your computer can include a range of useful features. Some may also be found on some Internet-based email services. The features include:

- Automatic filing of incoming email into folders so that you can keep things organised. Manual filing should also be possible.

- Managing groups of email addresses so you can send emails to more than one person at a time. This could be really useful if you have a group of people with which you need to communicate regularly such as a sports team you are in, a committee you are a member of, or a set of friends you tend to see as a group.

- Storing of pre-written phrases or draft emails. If you send emails with similar content on a regular basis, you may be able to save these as templates, which you can then use time after time as the basis for emails. This can be quite a time-saver.

- Signature files. If there is information you like to append to many emails, such as your address and phone number, you can save a special 'signature' which can be automatically appended to any email you choose.

- Email contact lists. Email software can also manage lists of contacts, separately from your main contacts list, if that is useful to you.

?

Did you know?

If you use email software on your laptop to collect email from one or more addresses, you should be able to set it to automatically send and receive messages at set intervals. If you have an always on, broadband Internet connection, this can be especially useful.

Email (cont.)

What comes with your operating system?

Windows XP comes with Outlook Express for managing email. In Windows Vista you get an application called Windows Mail for this job. The Mac OS also includes email software called Mail. Windows 7 does not include an email program.

What's free?

Some free alternatives are:

- Thunderbird (*www.mozilla.com/thunderbird*). Thunderbird is free email software from the same stable as the Firefox Web browser.

- Opera (*www.opera.com*). The Opera Web browser includes an email module which sits alongside the Web browser mentioned above.

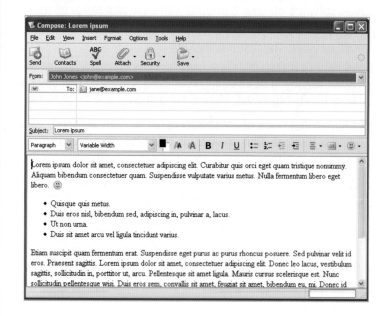

It is increasingly popular for people to use their computers to manage music and there are two ways in which you can do this:

- Download music from an online service and save it on your computer ready to copy across to mobile devices such as phones or portable music players.
- 'Rip' your own music from CD and store it on your computer.

Again it is possible to transfer this music to portable players or mobile phones. The process of ripping is straightforward, and many people find it convenient to have their music collection readily to hand in this way.

Music files can be stored in a number of different formats, and not all are playable on every device, so if you intend to use your laptop to store music and have a portable music player or mobile phone in mind, make sure that the format(s) you choose to use with the former are compatible with the latter.

There are many formats for mobile music. Here are some of the more popular ones you are likely to come across:

- AAC: this is the format preferred by Apple in its iTunes service and supported by its iPod and other music playing hardware.
- MP3: this is the most popular format for downloading music.
- OGG: this is a format popular with enthusiasts for its small file size but not widely supported by music players.
- WAV: this is a format which is less often used today for music as it saves relatively large files.
- WMA: this is a file format that is owned by Microsoft.

Different file formats have different characteristics. All the formats mentioned here 'compress' the original music in some way or another and this can result in the loss of some audio quality. Some audiophiles vastly prefer some formats over others.

Whatever you choose to use as your preferred format, files can be quite large. As well as taking account of the inherent qualities of the various music file formats you can rip music to

Jargon buster

Rip: the process of transferring media such as music from a standalone medium such as a music CD to your computer where it can be stored and/or moved to a personal media player.

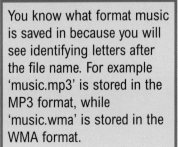

For your information

You know what format music is saved in because you will see identifying letters after the file name. For example 'music.mp3' is stored in the MP3 format, while 'music.wma' is stored in the WMA format.

Music (cont.)

Did you know?

?

Your mobile phone or music player may have a slot for a flash memory card (SD, miniSD, microSD and Memory Stick are the common formats for these). Your laptop may have a slot for reading from and writing to these cards. If it does not, you can purchase a reader which attaches to your laptop by USB. Using either method you will be able to manually copy files across to the card to listen to in a phone or music player. Check the device manual to find out if you need to put files into a specific folder in the memory card in order for your portable music player or phone to find them.

different audio qualities within a format depending on what you feel you need.

The quality you choose will affect the file size. There can be considerable variation here, but the general rule is that whatever format you choose, the better the quality, the larger the file is likely to be. A good audio quality MP3, for example, will need roughly 1 MB to 1.5 MB of file storage for every minute of music.

Getting music files from your computer to a portable music player or mobile phone should be straightforward. You may have as many as four different options – or a mix of them. You should take a look at the instructions that came with your device to check on the method(s) suggested.

Your portable music player or phone may have come with some music management software of its own. This may allow you to 'rip' and organise music, play it on your laptop and download it to your mobile device. If your device can't cope with the large file sizes you like to store on your laptop (for improved audio quality), the software may be able to automatically reduce the quality and file size as it transfers music across, saving you the time and bother of doing this job manually.

Much music management software that sits on your laptop for ripping, organising and playing music files lets you 'synchronise' players with your laptop. You choose the music you want to copy across, and the synchronisation process happens automatically from then on. Check the software you are using on your laptop to see what its features are.

Your mobile phone or music player may work in 'USB mass storage mode'. This means that when it is connected to your laptop via a USB cable its storage space will appear as if it were a hard drive. You can treat this space as if it were a drive on your laptop, using copy and paste or drag and drop to transfer files across. You can copy music files across in this way as well as using the player to transfer other files between computers as you see fit.

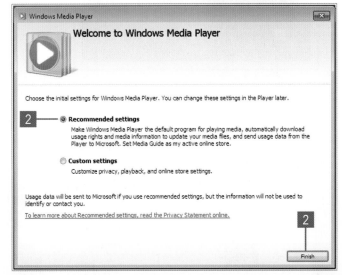

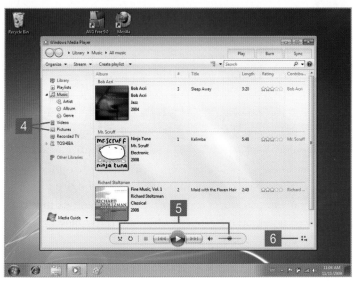

Use the Windows Media Player in Windows 7

1 Click Start then hover the cursor over All Programs and a list will appear from which you can choose Windows Media Player.

2 The first time you will need to choose a set-up. Choose Recommended settings by clicking to select that, then choose Finish.

3 The player will automatically import any media it finds on your computer, and these will be a few sample items for you to experiment with.

4 Windows Media Player opens in the music library. Choose other libraries such as Videos and Pictures from the list on the left.

5 To play an item double-click it. There are controls along the bottom of the window for volume, pause/play, skipping tracks, shuffle and repeat.

6 Use Now Playing mode to switch to a smaller view that offers minimal information and leaves more of the screen available for other tasks.

Music (cont.)

7 Click the Switch to Library button at the top right of the window to go back to the full Windows Media Player windows.

Create a playlist in the Windows 7 Windows Media Player

1 With the Windows Media Player opened click the Play tab in the top right corner.

2 Drag items from the main window over to the new right-hand pane which has appeared.

3 The number of items and total playing time will be shown at the bottom of this new pane.

4 When you are happy with the list click Save list and give your new playlist a name.

5 It will now be listed in the Playlists in the far left-hand window.

Many of the comments above apply to video as well as to music. You can transfer video to your computer from a handheld video camera, and can download video to your computer over the Internet. Many portable players can play video, allowing you to take it with you as you travel without your laptop.

You can also edit video on your laptop, so you can make your home movies look more professional, tying together sequences of shots into a movie you can show to other people.

Video can consume even more hard drive space than music, and so if you are going to be keen on storing video long term on your laptop you should take this into account when choosing a hard drive size.

What comes with your operating system?

Windows 7, XP and Vista come with the Windows Media Player which allows you to rip CDs, manage music lists, play music and synchronise with your portable player or mobile phone. It can handle other media too such as video. The Mac OS also includes its popular music management software iTunes.

What's free?

Some free alternatives are:

■ iTunes (*http://www.apple.com/itunes/download/*).
Apple's music manager is available for Windows XP, 7 and Vista as well as the Mac OS.

■ RealPlayer Basic (*http://uk.real.com*).

■ Winamp (*www.winamp.com*).

Video

Timesaver tip

If you intend to store music or video on your laptop hard drive consider the amount you are likely to want to store. You may find it useful to invest in a large hard drive from the outset, because you can't readily upgrade the hard drive on a laptop computer (see Chapter 5 for more on upgrading).

Video (cont.)

Many people have digital cameras, and the ideal way to store photos taken with a digital camera is to put them onto your hard drive. You will then be able to run slideshows, choose specific photos to show to people, and send photos to Internet services for printing.

Most digital cameras come with a range of software for organising, sorting, editing, viewing and printing images. You don't have to use this software, though, and there is a positive army of alternative software available, some of it free.

There is a great deal you can do with photos once they are on your computer. For example:

- store and archive
- organise into folders and files by criteria like theme, date, subject
- share with others over the Internet, for example by emailing them or by uploading to photo sharing sites
- display on your computer individually or as slideshows
- 'stream' to other devices: if you have a wireless network (see Chapter 4) you can make your photos accessible to any computer on the network
- bring together in new and different combinations on CDs for distribution to other people
- edit and manipulate to create new, different and exciting images
- use in publications such as newsletters or on the Web.

Being organised

With film cameras photos come at a premium – each one has to be individually developed, and you have to wait until a roll of film is finished before seeing the results. But with a digital camera you can take as many shots as you like and view them immediately on the camera's screen and then very soon afterwards on the larger screen of your laptop.

Because of this you can easily end up with hundreds of photos on your laptop very quickly.

Photos

6

Important

If you use photos in publications such as newsletters or on the Web then you *must* ensure you are the copyright owner or you have permission from the copyright owner for this kind of activity.

The easiest way to make sure you only have photos you want to keep on your laptop is to have an 'editing' session soon after you've taken the photos. If you have been on a day out maybe the session could be a couple of days after that; if you have been on holiday then editing a couple of days after your return is a good idea. Don't leave it too long or you may forget why you took a photo or what is in it.

There are two key things to do in an editing session. First of all, delete photographs you don't want. Perhaps because:

- they are out of focus
- it is not clear what the photo is actually of
- you took several photos of the same thing and want to keep only the best one(s)
- you were experimenting with an idea and it didn't work.

Secondly, make sure the photos you keep are properly annotated. The computer will record the date the photos were taken, but you might want to add a text description. Do it soon after the photos were taken so you don't forget what the pictures are actually of.

Even if you go through this process you are likely to amass many more photos than you would with an old film camera. And why not? It is fun to take photos and gather memories of an occasion. But if you are to get back to the photos again later you need to find a way of being organised.

The temptation is to try to handle this by getting a lot of photograph management software. This is fine if you get different software to do different tasks, but do take care as it can also cause confusion and unnecessarily clutter up your hard drive.

Getting prints

One further thing you can do with digital photos, just as with film-based photos, is to get prints. There are high-street stores which will produce prints from your camera's flash memory cards, or you could print your own with a photo-printer (we look at these in Chapter 7).

Alternatively you can use one of the many online services. The process is simple: sign up, upload your photos, decide what kind of prints you want, order. The websites advise on whether your images are of a high enough quality for the size of print you want.

Prints can be ordered in very small quantities and delivered to any address you choose. The process is usually very quick, and you can often order a large array of different kinds of products including T-shirts, mugs, cards, coasters, calendars, booklets and much more. Online print services also often offer you the opportunity to create albums of photos that other people can view – and order prints from.

What comes with your operating system?

Windows Vista comes with the Windows Photo Gallery, with which you can view, organise and share photos, and Windows Paint, a simple drawing utility which can be used as a basic picture editor. Windows XP comes with Windows Picture and Fax Viewer, which allows you to view images, and Paint, which can be used as a basic image editor. Windows 7 comes with Windows Photo Viewer and Paint. The Mac OS comes with iPhoto for viewing and editing photos.

What's free?

Some free alternatives are:

- Picasa (*www.picasa.google.com*)
- Gimp (*www.gimp-win.sourceforge.net*)
- Paint.NET (*www.getpaint.net*).

And two that offer free online image editing are:

- Splashup (*http://www.splashup.com*)
- Photoshop Express (*http://www.photoshop.com/express*).

Photos (cont.)

Look at photos with Windows Photo Viewer in Windows 7

1 When you double-click on a photo file it opens in the Windows Photo Viewer.

2 Use the buttons beneath the screen to zoom, rotate images, go backwards and forwards through pictures and see a slideshow.

3 Use the buttons at the top to print and email images and to burn them onto a CD.

We have left backing up to the last activity in this chapter, but that does not mean it is the least important. In fact, it is the most important thing you can do.

If you have read through the rest of this chapter and thought about all the things you can do with your laptop, including all the information you can store on it, from personal letters and financial planning to music, photos, email and other materials, you will realise that your computer can be a home to a vast amount of information that is important to both your personal and working life.

Imagine how dreadful it would be if you lost any of that information. Now imagine how dreadful it would be if you lost *all* of it.

Without wanting to be too alarmist, there are many ways in which you can suffer problems with your computer that can lead to data loss.

■ Data corruption. It can happen that individual files can get corrupted – rendered unreadable. There are many reasons that this can happen, but whatever the cause, it can be anything from mildly irritating to a complete disaster.

■ Hard drive failure. Hard drives are mechanical objects, and as such they can simply break. The hard drives in laptops tend to be cushioned against the knocks that a laptop has to take, but nonetheless it is unwise to fail to realise that they are relatively delicate items. If the hard drive fails it is likely that your laptop won't even switch on, so getting the data from the drive will be a task involving expensive data recovery services – and there is no guarantee you will get it all back.

■ Loss or theft. Lose your laptop, or have it stolen, and your data is gone for ever.

The key here is to make sure that you have adequate backups of everything that is important to you. There are several ways you can do this:

■ back up to an external hard drive

■ back up using an online service

■ make copies of important documents regularly to an external medium such as a CD-ROM.

Backing up
(cont.)

If you really want to back up thoroughly you need to be very organised. For example, ensure that you have more than one backup of all your data and that you check each one regularly. If files on your hard drive become corrupted and you copy them to a backup, the copies will be corrupted too, so you need to make sure that you are not simply backing up bad data.

> ### Timesaver tip
>
> It is also a good idea to store some backups in a different place to your laptop. If the laptop is stolen through a house burglary, for example, and you back up to an external hard drive, the thieves could steal the hard drive as well. At the very least consider storing a backup in a different part of your home, and at best consider storing it in another location, for example with a friend, neighbour or relative.

What comes with your operating system?

Windows 7, XP and Vista come with System Restore which while not strictly speaking a backup tool, allows you to backtrack after installing new software. This can be handy if an installation causes problems with the smooth running of your computer.

Windows 7 has two backup systems. File Backup allows you to make copies of the files you have created such as documents, photos, music or videos. You can choose precisely what to back up and save your backups to external devices.

System image backup makes a complete copy of the entire hard drive including:

- the Windows operating system
- any programs you have installed
- any settings you have made
- any data you have saved.

Windows Vista also includes a backup utility, though what you get depends on what version of Vista you have. Automatic File Backup comes with versions except Starter, and has basic functions in Home Basic edition. It helps you back up files.

Complete PC Backup is available in the Business, Ultimate and Enterprise editions of Vista. It makes a complete copy of your computer rather than just your files.

What's free?

A free alternative is:

- SyncBack (*http://www.2brightsparks.com*).

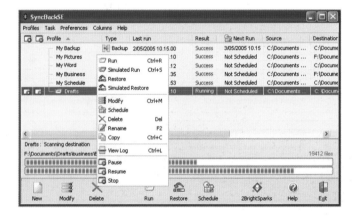

Did you know?

SyncBackSE is a powerful but easy to use backup, restore and synchronisation program.

Backing up (cont.)

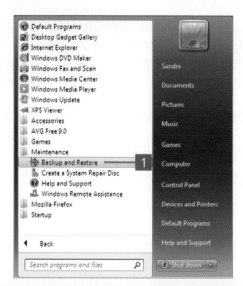

Back up your files in Windows 7

1. Click Start then hover the cursor over All Programs and a list will appear from which you can choose Maintenance and then Backup and Restore.

2. The first time you do this you will see a message saying 'Windows Backup has not been set up'. Click Set up backup.

3. When Windows Backup has started it will list all available devices and how much space there is on them. If you have an external hard drive connected this will be shown as an option.

4. Choose where you want the backup to go by clicking it, then click Next.

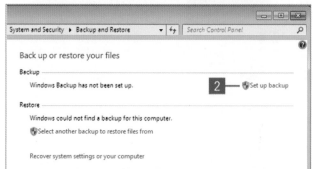

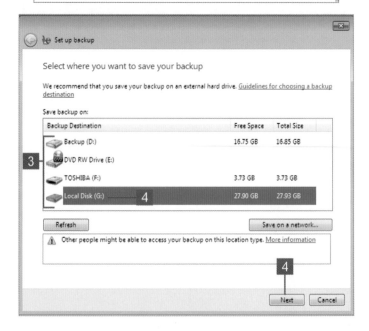

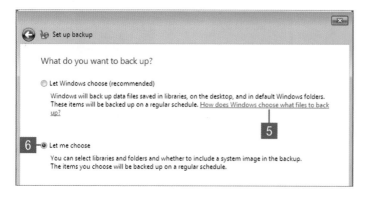

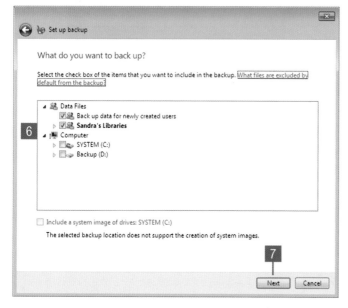

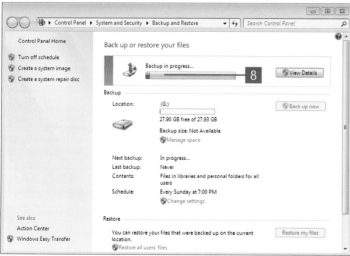

5 Now decide what you want to back up. Letting Windows choose will mean that files stored in default folders like Documents and Pictures will be backed up, but it won't include any separate folders you have created. Click 'How does Windows choose what files to back up?' to learn more.

6 If you opt for 'Let me choose' you can select precisely what should be backed up.

7 Either way, when you click Next you can set up a schedule for the backup by clicking Change Schedule, then choose Save settings and run backup.

8 The first backup will take place immediately.

Peripherals

7

Introduction

Much of the time you may find that your laptop functions perfectly well as a self-contained unit. You can add to the range of features it has when you first buy it by purchasing additional software to build on what it can do, as we have discussed in Chapter 6.

Another way to build on its capabilities is to use external devices to give it more scope. The ports and connectors on your laptop are designed precisely for this purpose. Depending on your needs and interests you may find a wide range of additional hardware which can build on what your computer can do.

In this chapter we consider some of the many peripherals you may wish to use to augment the features of your laptop.

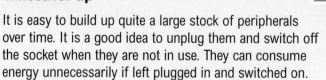

Timesaver tip

It is easy to build up quite a large stock of peripherals over time. It is a good idea to unplug them and switch off the socket when they are not in use. They can consume energy unnecessarily if left plugged in and switched on.

External keyboard and mouse

The keyboard on your laptop could be very large or very small depending on the overall size of the machine itself. In some of the largest laptops there may even be space for a separate number pad, as found on conventional keyboards used with desktop computers.

When it comes to a mouse you are most likely to have a touchpad with a couple of buttons that act as left and right mouse buttons do, giving you access to options within software. There may also be a scroll button which duplicates the features of the scroll wheel on a mouse.

Some laptops also have a touchstick, usually sitting between three keys on the keyboard, which can be used like a mini joystick.

Some people find these are perfectly adequate for their use, and never want to use alternatives. However, there are many mice and keyboards you could add to your computer and good reasons for choosing to do so.

Comfort and ergonomics

You may find that you want a more 'ergonomic' option for the mouse and keyboard than your laptop offers.

Some keyboards are designed to allow for a more comfortable and natural hand position, and these can help prevent repetitive strain injuries developing.

These tend to have a curved arrangement of keys which encourage your hands to rest at a comfortable angle. They may also have some keys further indented than others in order to cater for the differing lengths of your fingers.

For your information

The Logitech Wave Keyboard is designed to be ergonomic and comfortable to use.

In addition, some mice are designed to help with comfort. Trackball mice, for example, are thought by some to be more ergonomically sound than standard mice. Trackball mice sit in a static location on your desk and have a ball which you move around with your fingers. This movement is tracked by sensors, and is equated to cursor movement on screen.

Style and looks

It is unlikely that you will get a keyboard or mouse supplied with your laptop. When they are supplied with PCs they can be rather dull and utilitarian. So some people choose to buy keyboards and mice because they add a certain style to things.

There are many options to choose from including flat and sleek keyboards that are designed to look stylish and/or minimalist.

For your information

The Logitech diNovo Edge Keyboard has some additional features on its right side.

External keyboard and mouse (cont.)

Use an external wireless keyboard

1. Take the external keyboard you have chosen to use and read the instructions carefully to make sure you understand the set-up procedure.

2. A wireless keyboard will include a USB dongle. You will need to insert this into a USB port on your notebook.

3. You will also need to insert batteries into the keyboard. Check the manual to find out how many are needed and where they should go.

4. The keyboard may have an on/off switch which will need to be turned on.

5. There may also be a software CD which allows the keyboard to be used for its more advanced features. Again check the manual to find out how to install this software and what it can offer.

Extra features

At its most basic a keyboard needs to provide you with a set of QWERTY keys, a number pad, a set of cursor controls, a few standard keys for performing regularly used functions and a set of function keys. But keyboards can provide a lot more than this by way of dedicated buttons and there are even different keyboards designed for people with different broad computing interests.

For example, some keyboards have specialist keys for controlling multimedia, such as running music playing software, getting onto the Internet, controlling system volume and so on. Other keyboards have specialist controls for games players and these can include programmable keys so that you can use one key to perform a sequence of actions you might use regularly in a game.

For your information

The Logitech G15 Keyboard has a range of buttons beyond those usually found on a keyboard including some designed specifically for controlling music playback.

Losing cables

For those who like to avoid clutter there are cordless keyboards and mice. These rely on radio to send information to your laptop, and you need a free USB slot to fit a receiver into.

If you are keen on drawing you could try a graphics tablet. This is a flat panel you write onto using a stylus. The idea is that you can use the tablet in a similar way to how you use pen and paper. With a little practice graphics tablets can be really useful if you like working with images on your laptop.

Timesaver tip

With so many different styles of mouse and keyboard on offer it is important that what you finish up using is comfortable for you. With that in mind it is sensible to try before you buy. When testing a mouse or keyboard, consider the full range of features. Usability is especially important.

A keyboard should feel comfortable under the fingers – the keys should not be a stretch to reach, they should press in a comfortable amount for you and neither be too soft nor offer too much resistance to your fingers.

A mouse should neatly fit whichever hand you intend to use it with and its buttons should fall comfortably under the relevant fingers. If you are choosing a mouse with its wheel on the upper side, make sure you find it comfortable to move the wheel about.

◀ **Graphics tablets**

For your information 7

A graphics tablet is ideal for those who like working on art or design projects.

Timesaver tip

Whatever keyboard you choose, you will find touch-typing is a lot easier on the hands than hunting around for keys. It will take a little time to learn to touch-type, but the rewards can be great. When you touch-type you can sit back in a more comfortable position, not looking at the keyboard but at the screen. You will find you will type more quickly and because you intuitively know where the keys are that you want to press, you will be able to think more clearly about what it is you are writing, rather than concentrating on the process of finding each letter you want to type in turn.

External monitor

Use an external monitor with Windows 7

1 First plug your external monitor into your laptop.

2 Next click Start then click Control Panel.

3 When the Control Panel opens choose Appearance and Personalisation, then choose Connect to an External Display.

4 You can click the Display and Resolution boxes to control the settings of each monitor independently, so you can set the maximum resolution for each one.

5 If you want to be able to use both monitors at once click Multiple Displays and choose Extend these displays.

Of course your laptop has a screen. But for some people an external monitor is a useful addition. There are many reasons why you might find an external monitor useful. Examples include:

- You are a keen games player and are likely to enjoy the more immersive experience you get from a larger and faster monitor.

- You are very interested in graphics such as managing and editing digital photographs or drawing, and a large monitor provides more screen area in which to view your work.

- You want to do a lot of website viewing and find a larger screen than your laptop offers can help you see more of a page at once. You may find this is particularly the case if you choose an ultraportable laptop with a small screen.

- You want to have several document windows open at the same time, and find it is difficult to fit everything in on the smaller screen of your laptop. Again, you may find this is particularly the case if you choose an ultraportable laptop with a small screen.

- In a work situation you might want to send a presentation or other information to an external monitor which is large and well positioned for several people to look at, rather than have them crowd around your laptop.

- You want to be sure you use good ergonomics when using your laptop, and have decided you prefer a desk-based monitor to other solutions for this as it means you sit in a more ergonomic position.

Using the internal display and an external monitor at the same time

You should check your laptop manual for the fine detail on this, but there is often a keyboard shortcut that lets you switch between using the external monitor, the internal one on your laptop, or indeed using both.

There are various reasons why you might want to use two monitors at once. Some examples are:

- Working with lots of documents. Suppose you want to do some research on the Web and have a working document open at the same time. Two monitors might allow you to dedicate one to the Web and the other to your working document.

- Heavy email use. If you have a lot of email to deal with you could dedicate one monitor to that and use the other for whatever other tasks you are working on at the moment.

For your information ⓘ 7

An external monitor can be useful if your laptop has a smaller screen or you want to view two separate screens of information at once.

Printing black and white text

Probably the most widespread external device bought for any computer, desktop or laptop is a printer. Printers allow you to get what is inside your laptop and only visible on screen out on paper, and as such they are for many people an essential peripheral.

There are different types of printer, each with its own particular uses. You may find that more than one is appropriate for your needs.

If your main needs are likely to be based around printing ordinary black and white text on plain paper, then your choices run between laser printers and inkjet. You may see inkjet printers offered at very aggressive prices and be drawn to one over the laser printer option.

However, laser printers do have some advantages. They can be quieter to run and while the initial cost might be more than for an inkjet printer, the ongoing running costs, in terms of buying toner, could be considerably lower than the cost of buying ink cartridges for an inkjet printer.

Inkjets may be more appealing to you if space is limited as they can be smaller than laser printers, and they also often print on a wider range of materials than laser printers. If you are interested in projects like T-shirt printing, or crafts which involve using card, then this may be appealing.

When choosing between an inkjet or laser printer it is important to consider the following questions:

- What will you use it for?
- How much space do you have?
- What is likely to be the total running cost? Compare the basic printer cost and its ink costs.

Some laser printers are very low in cost. Be aware that in some cases these are slow to run. If all you do is print single sheets such as letters then you may have no difficulty with them. But if you need to print longer documents, and particularly if you need to print documents at speed, for example if you want to print leaflets, such printers may prove frustrating to use.

Timesaver tip

Look for a printer that can automatically print on both sides of a sheet of paper. This is called 'duplex' printing. Over time it can save considerable money on printer paper, and it also gives you more flexibility in the format of your printed output.

Timesaver tip

Consider buying recycled printer paper. It is kinder to the environment and the quality of your printing should not suffer.

Printing in colour

If you want to produce colour prints, for example because you want to produce leaflets or your documents involve a lot of colour, then you could consider a colour laser printer. But these are still relatively expensive for the home user, with prices ranging far higher than the under £100 you will need to pay for a colour inkjet printer.

When looking for a colour printer it is again important to weigh up the cost of the printer itself and its ongoing running costs. You may find costs vary considerably and what looks like a very affordable printer at the point of purchase could turn out to be quite expensive to run in comparison with other printers because of the cost of ink cartridges.

The coloured inks used by colour printers are consumed in different amounts over time. This will vary depending on your printing tendencies, but it is very unlikely that you will use all colours in equal proportions.

With this in mind consider choosing a printer which uses separate cartridges for each colour of ink. That way you can replace each colour cartridge when it becomes empty. Printers which offer a 'combined' cartridge for their coloured inks are not economical as the whole cartridge needs to be replaced when one colour runs out. Inevitably this means that you throw away some ink without using it.

Timesaver tip

Printers give you a warning when ink is running low. Even if the warning suggests you should replace the cartridge or toner immediately you may not need to. So when you get the 'low ink' warning make sure you have a replacement ink source to hand, but consider waiting till you see visible signs of low ink in your printing before using it.

For your information

This photo and document printer, the Canon PIXMA iP4500, folds away neatly for storage.

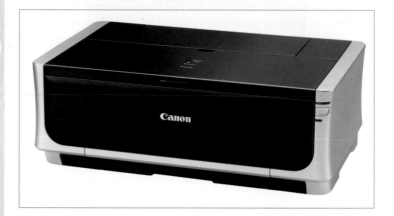

162

Photo printers are increasingly popular as they allow you to get quick prints from your digital camera. Even if you have a colour printer that is an inkjet or laser, a dedicated photo printer could be a good additional investment if you are keen on digital photography as they are specially designed to produce prints at photographic quality.

Photo printers can use up to six different colour cartridges. This might sound like a lot, but the use of more ink colours means the printer can get a finer gradation of colour and so produce prints that are of photographic quality. As with the advice on colour printing more generally, it is more economical to choose a printer with separate colour cartridge than one which combines colours in a single cartridge.

A photo printer really benefits from using special photographic paper. You will probably find that your printer manufacturer has its own brand paper. This is designed to work well with the manufacturer's branded ink. If you want to use another brand of paper, for example to save money, there is no technical reason not to. But you may find print quality is variable, so buy in smaller quantities and run tests before deciding on a longer-term solution.

Among the features that photo printers can offer is printing direct from a camera without the need of a computer and printing from a memory card. Both of these features can be useful if you want to print photos without having to use your computer as a 'go-between' between your camera and printer.

Printing photographs

7

For your information

This compact printer, the Canon Selphy ES20, specialises in printing photos.

Online printing services

An alternative to having your own photo printer is to use an online printing service. Typically these services accept photos uploaded to them over the Internet, and can provide prints posted to you within a working day or two.

Many services also offer online storage for your photos, which you can open up to others in order to share images with them.

Online printing services can produce prints at many sizes. Depending on the quality of your digital camera these could include prints at sizes larger than you would be able to produce at home with a photo printer. They also offer printing in a wide variety of styles and designs – again certainly more than you would be capable of achieving at home with a photo printer. For example, online printing services can produce things like calendars, notebooks, greetings cards, postcards, mugs, mousemats, coasters, jigsaw puzzles, T-shirts, photo booklets and more.

There are lots of reasons why you might want to print labels. Perhaps, for example, you are involved in a local club, society or charity, and need to print mailing labels from time to time. Or maybe you are involved in a craft such as making preserves and like to print your own labels to put onto jars.

You can purchase address labels on A4 sheets and use these with your ordinary printer. Or you could consider purchasing a special label printer. These are relatively small because they tend to print on labels one at a time from a roll.

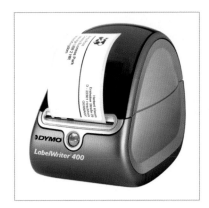

7

Dot matrix printers

The very first types of printer available were 'dot matrix' printers and they are still available today. Dot matrix printers are reliable and low cost to run. They print using a pattern of dots to make each individual character.

Dot matrix printers are much more likely to be found in a business setting than a home one today, and to be used for draft printing or for printing that is not intended for wide public use as the quality is poorer than it is with inkjet or laser printers.

If you use your laptop at different places around the home or office and would like to be able to print without having to make a physical connection between the laptop and printer using a cable, then you can consider wireless printing.

This could be useful if you want to be able to use your laptop at different places around the home or office and print from it wherever you happen to be. In addition, any computer with wireless capability can share use of the printer, so that several computers can use a single printer easily.

There are two options if you are interested in wireless printing. Both use the Wi-Fi standard. If you already run a wireless network, most probably because you want to have access to your Internet connection from anywhere in your home without being limited to locations where you have set up a wired link, then this could be appealing. (For more on wireless communications see Chapter 4.)

Built-in

You could buy a printer with wireless capability built into it. If you are keen on this, the range of printers you can choose between will be relatively small as built-in wireless is only found in a small number of printers. However, the advantage is that the wireless components are internal to the printer and so you don't have to find space for additional hardware.

Add-on

If you choose a printer without wireless capability built in, then you can add on a separate wireless 'print server'. This can communicate with your network and allow you to access the printer from any location within network range.

Did you know?

It is possible to connect a printer to a wireless network with a special add-on called a print server.

Scanners

Scanners are very versatile pieces of equipment. If you think of a printer as a tool for getting material that is on your laptop out and onto paper (or a similar material), then a scanner does the opposite. It takes material on tangible media and turns it into a format you can use on your computer.

Scanners can have a range of uses. For example:

- scanning photos so you can do a multitude of things with them, such as:
  - send them to other people by email
  - edit them individually or into montages
  - store them on your computer for safe keeping
  - make collections on CD or other media for storage and sharing
  - use them in print projects
- keeping records of important documents on your computer from bills and official letters to receipts that you might need to use for work-related expenses claims.

When used in conjunction with Optical Character Recognition (OCR) software scanners can be used to turn a text-based printed page into text that you can import into word processing software on your computer and from there edit or augment as needed.

When choosing a scanner it is important to think about the kinds of uses you will put it to. First off, consider the general format. There are several main types of scanner.

Flatbed scanner

This is by far the most common and popular type of scanner for the home user. It is easily recognised thanks to its flat plate onto which you put the object to be scanned, and a lid that covers the object. Flatbed scanners can vary in size, with the smallest not much larger than a sheet of A4 paper.

Did you know?
A scanner lets you store any paper-based document on your computer.

Sheetfeed or document scanner

As the name suggests this type of scanner is designed for scanning single sheets of paper. You will find them of little use for anything other than single sheets which can be fed through one at a time. They aren't ideal for home use for a number of reasons, including that they are only suitable for paper whereas it is possible to put non-flat items into a flatbed scanner.

Photo scanner

You can scan photographs using an ordinary flatbed scanner, but specialised photo scanners can give you a better quality image from original photographic images. You can also find photo scanners with specialist features for scanning slides. Some also come with software designed to help you touch up photographs such as removing scratch marks that are on the original image.

Handheld or pen scanner

Handheld scanners can look like a large marker pen and are designed for reading text a line at a time. They are suited to students or others who feel the need to scan a lot of information from magazine articles or books, but are not very flexible in terms of their range of uses.

Scanners (cont.)

Business card scanner

If you are the kind of person who meets a lot of new contacts and likes to keep their details on your computer, then a business card scanner could be of interest. These are designed to extract contact information from business cards and put that information into your contacts management software. They tend to be quite small. You could probably keep one in a drawer and just attach it to your computer when it is needed.

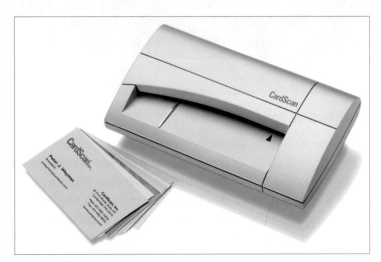

Points to consider when choosing a scanner

Scanning resolution

Scanners capture their image of the item to be scanned as a number of dots per inch. This can be expressed as either 'optical resolution' or 'interpolated resolution'. When noting what scanners can do always pay more attention to the optical resolution than the interpolated. The latter is produced using software and is enhanced from the former, which is therefore the best guide as to the native capability of the equipment.

There is a trade-off to be made between resolution and file size, as the more dots per inch there are in a scan, the larger the file will be. You can set the scanner to produce files that are smaller than the maximum it is capable of, and so can be flexible in the use of your scanner, which could be helpful for producing scans you want to store in the long term or use as elements of a website for example.

Colour depth

The higher the number quoted as colour depth, the more colour gradations the scanner can cope with. More is generally better, especially if you intend to scan colour rich materials like photographs.

Size

It is likely that you will want to scan A4 sheets of paper and so your scanner needs to be able to accommodate these with ease. Most flatbed scanners should be able to do this with no trouble, but if you are in any doubt, check.

7

All in one multi function devices

If space is limited you could consider an all in one device that can both print and scan. These devices are often referred to as multi function devices (MFDs). The printer side of these can be a laser printer or an inkjet. MFDs have their pros and cons. On the plus side the fact that scanner and printer are built into the same machine means that there is an extra function bolted on – a copier. If you need to make copies of things a lot and you do not have a handy corner shop with a good quality photocopier nearby, this could come in very handy.

Of course you can make copies with a separate scanner and printer too. You simply scan the item to your PC, and then print it out through your printer. But having both functions together in a situation where you only need to make minimal button presses could be useful.

Some MFDs can also act as a fax machine. Faxing is something that you can do direct from your laptop, but having this function in an MFD instead has its advantages. For example, imagine you download a form from the Internet or it is emailed to you. To fax it from your laptop you would need to print it, fill it in, scan it then fax it. To fax it from an MFD you can eliminate the need to scan it after you have filled it in.

Finally, if ports and connectors are limited on your laptop then you may be drawn by the fact that you only need a single connector for an MFD where you would need two for a separate printer and scanner. The same goes for mains power sockets. An MFD needs just one whereas a separate printer and scanner would need one each.

On the minus side these combined devices can be relatively large and so it is not always easy to find space for them in your home or home office. This becomes more relevant if you are not likely to need your scanner very much. Some people find they can put their scanner away in its box for much of the time, just getting it out on the odd occasions when it is needed for a task.

There is also the design issue. If the look of your IT equipment is important to you, then you will be pleased that you can find some printers which are rather neatly designed. However, the same is often not true of MFDs which tend to be somewhat blocky in design.

There is also a longer-term issue of maintenance to consider. With a separate scanner and printer, if one breaks for some reason, you only need to replace or repair a single device. If part of your MFD breaks then you may need to consider replacing the entire device. And you could be without any of the functions it offers until you organise a replacement or repair.

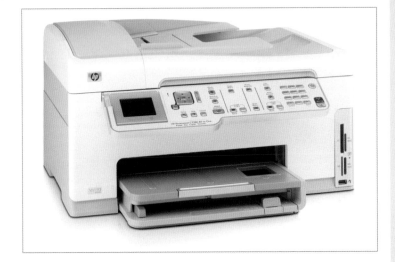

7

For your information

It might look complex but a device like this can print, copy, scan and fax and can save a lot of space when compared with having separate devices for each function.

Wireless modem and router

If you have a broadband Internet connection you will need a modem to enable you to use it. Your Internet Service Provider (ISP) may give you one of these as part of your contract. Alternatively you can buy one from a computer store.

The modem should be able to provide both wired (Ethernet) and wireless (Wi-Fi) access for several computers. (See Chapter 4 for more on this whole topic.)

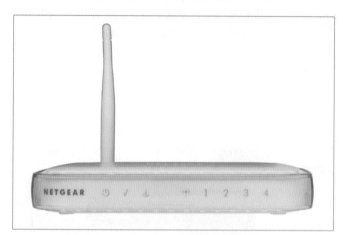

Did you know?

If you want to set up a wireless network then a router is an essential piece of kit.

Many laptops these days have readers for flash memory cards of the kinds found in digital cameras, mobile phones, some portable music players and other portable equipment.

Depending on your laptop you may have readers for any or all of the following card formats:

- Compact Flash
- SD (Secure Digital)
- MicroSD
- MiniSD
- xD
- Memory Stick
- Memory Stick Pro Duo
- Memory Stick Micro.

If you have a built-in reader for the card types you like to use, then all you need to do is insert the card into the reader and the card will appear as if it were an additional hard drive. To get to it you just need to double-click the My Computer icon on your desktop and then you can open the card, see its contents, copy and paste files to it, and delete files from it as you would with the hard drive of your laptop.

Memory card reader

Use a card reader with Windows 7

1. If you have a card reader that can accommodate multiple different kinds of flash memory cards, it will connect to your laptop via USB and will probably simply need to be plugged in to be recognised.

2. If that is the case (the manual will confirm it) plug the card reader into an available USB port on your laptop. You may notice some information appearing in the Notification Area at the bottom right of the screen as the laptop prepares to recognise the card reader.

3. You will now be able to insert cards into the card reader and then click Start and then Computer to see the cards listed under Devices with removable storage. You can click to open cards and view their contents, and copy files to and from them.

SDHC

SDHC cards are a relatively new addition to the flash memory card range. The term stands for Secure Digital High Capacity. Now that you know that you may not be surprised to learn that SDHC cards can store more data than standard ones. This is good news for those who need to store lots of data on such cards. Some modern digital cameras, media players, smartphones and other devices support these cards, which means you can carry more music, save more photos and so on with them.

However, they need a compatible reader. This will not be a problem if you buy a new laptop, but if you buy an older, possibly second-hand laptop, you may hit a problem.

If your laptop can't read SDHC format cards, you can get adaptors which allow your laptop to read the cards. These tend to slot into an available USB port.

Use an SD/SDHC card with Windows 7

1. Look for a port on your laptop that is the right size to take an SD card.

2. Put your card into the reader. You may notice some information appearing in the Notification Area at the bottom right of the screen as the laptop prepares to read your card.

3. Click Start and then click Computer.

4. You will see information about your hard drive as usual but your SD card will be listed under Devices with removable storage. You can click to open the card and view its contents, and copy files to and from it.

Timesaver tip

To find out if your laptop memory card reader can cope with SDHC cards without needing a separate reader, check for the use of the term SDHC in its specifications. If you are in doubt, ask before you buy your laptop.

If your laptop does not have a card reader built into it, or cannot read the card formats you want to use, then you can obtain an external card reader. Typically these fit into the USB port of your laptop.

There are many options. Some allow you to read a small number of card types, others can cope with many different card types.

Did you know?

A card reader can help you get data onto your laptop from many different memory card formats.

7

Webcam

You may think that video calling is only possible with 3G mobile phones, but in fact laptops can be used for video calls too. Video calls are best made from laptops over the Internet, and work best when you have a broadband Internet connection.

You'll need some additional software to help you make video calls. If you buy a webcam it should come with some software, and there may be some pre-loaded onto your laptop as well.

You can also download software from the Internet. Examples of free software include:

■ Skype from *www.skype.com*

■ Windows Live Messenger from *http://download.live.com*

■ Yahoo Messenger from *http://uk.messenger.yahoo.com*

Some laptops have built-in webcams which are ideal for this purpose. They generally sit above the screen in the frame area.

If your laptop does not have a built-in webcam there are many external ones to choose from, and they offer a strong range of added features beyond simply being able to send and receive video images over the Internet.

Webcam features can include:

- still image capture
- video capture
- automatic self-adjustment to take account of light and shade and provide a good quality image
- self-adjusting auto focus so that if you move away from or nearer to the camera it can automatically ensure you stay in focus
- face tracking so that if you move around while you are involved in a video call software will ensure the camera lens follows you so that you stay within the picture.

? 7

Did you know?

If your laptop doesn't have a built in webcam it is easy to add one.

Laptop stands

Some people find that working with a laptop sitting flat on their desk can be a little awkward, and they would like something which improves their comfort.

There are stands which can do this, both lifting the keyboard into a less flat position and lifting the screen higher too. Some stands even incorporate a separate keyboard so that your laptop can be positioned with its screen in a much higher position than would be possible if you wanted to use its keyboard.

Stands can make good sense from a user ergonomic point of view as they encourage you to sit with better posture.

It is very important that you keep the contents of your laptop backed up. If you do not protect the contents of your laptop from loss, damage or theft then if the worst happens you could lose vital data. See Chapter 8 for more information on this.

One way to ensure your data is safe against mishaps is to back it up to an external hard drive. The drive can be stored in a different location to your laptop when you are not making the backup.

External hard drives have other uses too. For example, you may have more than one computer in the home and want to share information between them. Examples might include family photographs, digital copies of your own music or important documents such as family finance records or vital letters.

You could share the contents of your laptop with other computers over your Wi-Fi network, but there is a significant snag with doing this. Your laptop has to be switched on for others to have access to the contents of its hard drive.

Using an external hard drive to provide this kind of access could be a better solution. The drive can always be on, and so always accessible. It can be connected to your Wi-Fi network so that others on the network can use it. And it could even be set up so that you can access it remotely, when you are away from home.

And there is another possible use for an external hard drive. Imagine you take lots of digital photos and like to share them with friends and family. One option would be to take your laptop with you when you visit and use its screen to display them. But another would be to take an external hard drive instead, plug that into their computer, and display the photos from there.

If you are thinking of carrying data around in this way then look around for small-sized, so-called 'portable', external hard drives. Typically these are small and light to carry – and could even fit into your pocket.

External hard drive

7

External hard drive (cont.)

USB flash drives are a very useful peripheral. They plug into any available USB port and you can then copy data onto them and carry it around with you. Because USB ports are found on every laptop, you are guaranteed to be able to access your data from any computer.

USB flash drives are thus useful in a wide range of situations where you want access to data of some kind but don't want to carry your laptop. For example:

■ You are going to visit friends or relations and want to show them some photos you took on holiday. Carry them on a flash drive and use their computer to view the photos.

■ You are travelling for a work meeting and want to deliver a presentation on a laptop. Carry the presentation on a flash drive, making sure the laptop you want to use has compatible software on it.

■ You are working on a report or document but don't want to carry a computer around when you know there are computers you can use at your destination. Put the report and any associated documents onto a USB flash drive and carry that to your destination instead.

USB flash drives are 'plug and play' devices. This means that when you plug one into the USB port on a computer it will be recognised automatically and show up as a drive which you can access. You can copy files to and from it, and open files that are stored on it, all without needing to install any extra software.

U3 drive

USB flash drives can be used for more than just accessing applications. A type of drive called U3 can run applications too. You can install applications like word processors and Web browsers onto a U3 compliant USB flash drive, and then put that into a computer and run software from it.

This can be very useful if you want to do things like carry a Web browser and some bookmarks around with you, or be certain that you will have access to a word processor you know how to use on any computer.

USB flash drive

7

Important

When using a USB flash drive to access your files on another computer you need to be sure that the computer on which you want to use the drive has software which can read the file types you want to access.

For your information

You can find out more about U3 drives at *www.U3.com*.

Important

U3 is a specific type of USB flash drive. If you are interested in trying it out you must buy a USB flash drive that is U3 compatible.

USB flash drive (cont.)

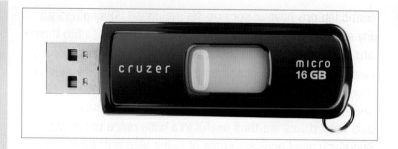

Did you know?

USB drives can be used to store information you might need to move from one laptop to another.

Some laptops have a 'docking station' as an optional extra. Essentially this is a separate unit which connects to the laptop and provides a range of ports and connectors.

In some cases the docking station offers more connectors of different types than the laptop itself does. This could particularly be the case if you have chosen an ultraportable laptop which can be very small and therefore not have much space for connectors around its edges.

If you have an area set aside for computing where a scanner, printer and other peripherals are permanently sited, then a docking station offers an important advantage. You can leave all your peripherals plugged into it, and then connect it to your laptop via a single connector.

This not only saves you time when you want to take your laptop away with you or reconnect it to the rest of your equipment, it can help protect the connectors on the laptop as they are not constantly having peripherals connected and disconnected.

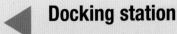

Docking station

For your information

Docking stations add an array of additional ports and connectors to a laptop. They fit onto the back of the laptop where they are relatively unobtrusive.

USB hub

Many peripherals connect to a computer via USB. This is a standard type of connector found on all computers. Laptops incorporate different numbers of USB connectors. The smallest ultraportable laptops might have just two USB connectors, while larger laptops could have four or even six.

Depending on the laptop you buy and the number of peripherals you want to use, you may not have enough USB connectors to connect them all at once. The simple solution to this dilemma is to buy a USB hub.

A USB hub is also a good idea if you move your laptop around frequently. It is better to plug multiple devices that stay in one location into a hub than into your laptop for several reasons:

- It can save you time. You can leave the devices, such as your printer, scanner, external keyboard and mouse, permanently plugged in, and just plug the one connector – the one to the USB hub – into your laptop when needed.

- It can help keep things tidy. If all your peripherals are plugged into a USB hub you can deal with trailing wires just once, ensuring they are all neat and tidy on your desk. If you plug things into your laptop every time you want to use it, the wires may not always be neat and tidy.

- It can help protect the connectors on your laptop. However careful you are, frequent use of connectors on your laptop can jar and maybe damage them.

A single USB hub can provide up to seven ports, so that you can connect seven peripherals to a single USB connector. USB hubs come in a wide range of shapes and sizes, and some even connect to your laptop wirelessly. This can be really useful if you like to use your computer away from the desk on which the USB hub sits, but still want access to the peripherals connected to it.

We have even come across a mouse with two USB connectors built into it. This could be useful if you know you need extra USB connectors when you are carrying your laptop around and do not want to carry a USB hub separately.

?

Did you know?

If your laptop does not have enough USB ports you can add more with a USB hub.

?

Did you know?

This mouse has its own built-in USB hub.

Spare battery

A laptop computer is designed to survive on its own battery. Sometimes you may find yourself needing more time away from mains power than the provided battery can supply. In these instances it could be handy to have a second battery.

Most laptops have removable batteries, and you can fit a spare one in the same slot.

If you want to consider buying a second battery, check what is on offer. There may be more than one option for your laptop. For example, there may be a higher-capacity, longer-life battery available.

If there is a higher-capacity battery option it is likely to be larger than the standard battery, and will therefore make your laptop a little heavier than with the standard battery.

If you intend to carry your laptop around then it deserves to have good protection. There are many bags designed specifically for carrying laptops. Typically they have the following characteristics:

- a padded area for your laptop to provide it with good protection against bumps and knocks
- separate sections for power supplies, wires and other paraphernalia
- additional sections for other materials you may need to carry, for example paperwork or even overnight clothes.

There are many different types of laptop bag.

Traditional case

Briefcase style cases that can be carried in the hand or over the shoulder are a popular type of bag among business users. They can be made of soft materials or have a hard outer case.

Shoulder bags/messenger bags

Designed to be rather more funky than traditional briefcase type bags these are available in a range of attractive styles.

Backpacks

Backpacks are a great idea as they distribute the weight of your laptop evenly over the back. There are many distinctive designs and they tend to have a range of pockets so that you can carry cables and connectors separately as well as other non-computing materials.

Trolleys

Like flight bags, trolleys are often on wheels and have built-in extending handles. They can be quite large, enabling you to carry both your laptop and standard luggage of the type you might need if going on a trip for a weekend. Many are of an appropriate size to take onto an airplane as hand luggage.

Laptop sleeves

There are many designs of laptop sleeve. They range from zip-around cases made of soft material such as neoprene and

Backpack or carrying case

7

Backpack or carrying case (cont.)

designed in a variety of colours to envelope-style cases with flip-over lid sections. They can be useful if you want to carry a laptop in a bag that lacks a special padded area as they provide the padding, but be aware that some provide more protection against knocks and bangs than others.

Timesaver tip

Ergonomics and health: Think about how often you are likely to carry your laptop, in what circumstances, and how heavy it is likely to be.

Timesaver tip

Safety first: When choosing a laptop bag consider the safety issue. Some laptop bags look precisely like what they are. These may be a giveaway to a potential thief that you are carrying a laptop. Consider choosing a bag type and design that looks less like a laptop case and more like an ordinary bag, and you could help to deter opportunistic thieves.

Over the shoulder bags are not necessarily an ideal option, especially for heavy laptops or when you need to keep your hands free.

Rucksacks are great for distributing weight around your body evenly, and they leave both hands free which could be useful in a range of situations. For example, if you commute and want to visit a food store on the way home a rucksack leaves both hands free for carrying what you buy.

Laptop security I: authorising access and backing up

Introduction

When we think about laptop security we are really thinking about two distinct types of security: the information you store and create, and the ways in which people are able to access your laptop. Both are equally important.

You need to take good care that the information stored on your computer is safe and secure, and we will look at that in this chapter.

You also need to take precautions to protect access to your Internet connection and, if you have more than one computer that you link together, to the network they form. We will look at that in the next chapter.

Once you have had a laptop for a few months it is likely you will be using it for all sorts of tasks. Some you may have planned from the very start, others may have developed in a natural way as you discover more and more about your laptop's capabilities, or maybe as you realise you could use it to help realise some long-held ambitions.

However it came about, it is likely that you have 'data' on your laptop that is important to you and that you want to protect.

In some instances this may be data you want to keep safe from prying eyes. In other cases it might be data that you just want to be sure is not going to disappear by accident one day because it is not duplicated anywhere else.

There are all kinds of things that you might have on your computer which are precious to you in some way either as personal information or as information you want to ensure is always accessible.

For example data could include:

- documents of all types and ranging from official to personal communications
- music that you may have bought from an online store or copied from your own music CDs
- photos and videos – if you have a digital camera or video recorder it is surprising how quickly you can amass a store of images that is not replicated elsewhere
- bookmarks in your Web browser – after just a few months of having a computer it is likely you will have amassed quite a collection of bookmarks of favourite websites
- records of your contacts or friends such as might be stored in a contacts database
- email you may have exchanged with people that could contain important information you do not want to lose.

If you are to protect such information and more you need to take measures to ensure its security, and measures to ensure that if the worst happens and you lose access to your laptop for some reason, you still have copies of the data.

For your information

'Data' is a term used to describe any kind of information stored on a computer hard disk. It could be a document, photo, video file, even an application. Everything, in fact, on your computer is data of one sort or another.

It is possible to set up your laptop so that only you or a selection of people you authorise are allowed to access it. You can do this by setting up user accounts complete with their own passwords.

There are three key benefits to having user accounts:

- **Personalisation**. Individual users can set up the computer to look different depending on each one's needs. A user can have their own image on the main screen of the laptop, and shortcuts to their preferred applications there too.

- **Sharing and not sharing files**. Data stored on the laptop can be designated as either shared or not, and if it is not shared other users can't see it.

- **Access to controls**. You can limit the degree of access to features that particular users have. You can see immediately how this can be a great help with regard to protecting access to sensitive files and system configuration.

Imagine that one laptop is shared by the whole family. The adults will need access to documents like family accounting information, banking details and important official documents. The children should definitely not be given access to this information. Setting up the system with a range of user accounts for each family member means you can control who has access to what.

Types of user accounts

There are different kinds of user account in Windows and the type of account an individual is assigned dictates the sort of things they can do.

Windows 7 offers three types of user accounts:

- **Administrator account**. Administrator accounts have access to everything on the laptop. Anyone logged on as an administrator can install applications, access files, manage other users, delete files and folders and so on. Someone with an administrator account can add other user accounts and change their settings.

- **Standard account**. Someone with a standard account can exercise a lot of controls, such as deciding which desktop wallpaper they want and what shortcuts they want on the

User accounts (cont.)

desktop, but they can't make any changes that affect other accounts.

- **Guest account**. The guest account is a very limited access account that is useful for people who make temporary use of a computer, for example a houseguest who just wants to do a few tasks like check their email.

In Windows Vista there are also three types of user accounts:

- **Administrator account**. Very similar to administrator accounts in Windows 7.

- **Standard user account**. Very similar to standard accounts in Windows 7.

- **Guest account**. Very similar to guest accounts in Windows 7.

In Windows XP there are three types of user accounts:

- **Administrator account**. Very similar to administrator accounts in Windows 7.

- **Limited user accounts**. Very similar to standard accounts in Windows 7.

- **Guest accounts**. Very similar to guest accounts in Windows 7.

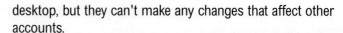

For your information

When you set up a user account you need to tell the computer what kind of user they will be. This controls the level of access they have to the computer, barring some from being able to make system level changes.

Timesaver tip

In Windows Vista Home Basic, Home Premium and Ultimate you can set up parental controls, making limits to the games playing, Web access and computer use that different users have. This feature is not available in Windows Vista Business.

Timesaver tip

You can have more than one account of a type. So in a house with adults and children, the adults could all have an Administrator account, the children all Limited user or Standard user accounts. Each person can have an account with their own name attached to it, or several users could share an account. When a visitor comes to stay, they can use your computer as a Guest.

Did you know?

You can set up login passwords for different users.

User accounts (cont.)

Set up a user account in Windows 7

1. Click Start and choose the Control Panel.

2. Next choose Add or remove user accounts.

3. At the bottom of the next screen click on Create a new account.

4. Give the account a name.

5. Decide which of the two account types it should have. An Administrator has full access to the computer while a Standard user has less control and this is the type of account that most people should be given.

6. When you have selected an account type click Create Account.

7. That user will now appear on the list of users and will be able to log on to the computer when it starts up.

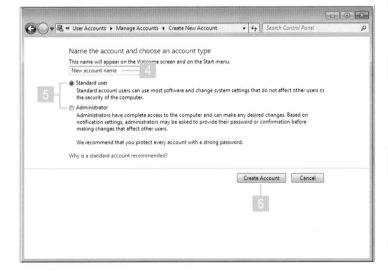

8

User accounts (cont.)

Set up a password for a user in Windows 7

1. Click Start and choose the Control Panel.

2. Next click User Accounts and Family Safety. (If you are an Administrator you will be able to edit the information for all users by clicking Manage another account.)

3. Now choose Change your Windows Password.

4. Choose Create a Password for this account.

5. Next type the password. You'll need to type it twice, to confirm that you typed what you really wanted the first time. Make sure it is memorable as it will need to be used by whoever it has been created for (you or another user) when they log on.

6. Type a password hint.

7. Finally, click Create password.

If you are in a household with children then you may be concerned about how they could use the Internet. It is possible to restrict their access using parental control software. This type of software typically either monitors or blocks access to material deemed unsuitable.

The sorts of things this software can do include:

- blocking access to known websites
- restricting Internet chat sessions so that personal information can't be divulged
- logging keystrokes, which is useful for various monitoring activities such as capturing login passwords your children may use for websites
- monitoring email
- keeping an eye on whatever is typed
- blocking access to specified software on your PC
- setting scheduled time periods which limit computer users both online and offline
- producing activity reports so you can monitor what other users have been doing.

Examples of software you can try include:

- Net Nanny at *http://www.netnanny.com*
- CyberPatrol at *http://www.cyberpatrol.com*
- Shield Plus at *http://www.guardware.co.uk*
- CYBERSitter at *http://www.cybersitter.com*.

Parental control software

Timesaver tip

Parental control software can be a very useful part of a family computer. But consider its use in a rounded way. You might feel it is appropriate to tell household members that you are using this software, rather than simply using it surreptitiously.

8

Parental control software (cont.)

Change the parental controls in Windows 7

1. Click Start and choose the Control Panel.

2. Choose Set up parental controls for any user. Note that you only have access to this if you have an Administrator level user account.

3. Click the account you want to set up parental controls for.

4. Click the On button so that the greyed out options all become accessible.

5. Choose Time limits.

6. On the next screen you can set the times at which the user is allowed to use the laptop and time at which access is blocked.

7. Choose Games.

8. On the next screen you can set limits on whether games can be played at all and control access to specific games.

9. Choose Allow and block specific programs.

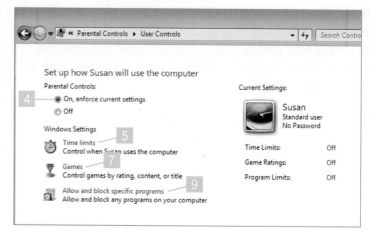

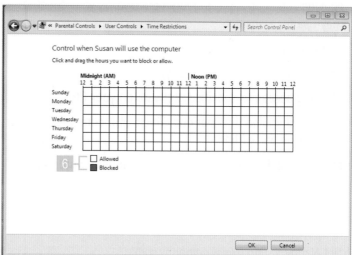

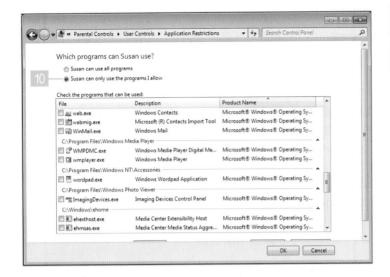

10 On the next screen choose only to let the user access programs you allow.

11 On the next screen you can choose specific programs that can be used by checking them off from a list.

8

Fingerprint recognition

Fingerprint recognition is a biometric security device in that it is based on a biological trait. Fingerprints are unique – this is why they are used by the police to help identify people.

Some laptops have fingerprint recognition built in. Its use in computers is designed to help ensure security because only the person possessing the fingerprint that a computer recognises will be allowed to log on and use the computer.

You can tell if a computer has this feature because there is a small fingerprint scanner somewhere on the casing. Often this is found near the keyboard, sometimes near the touchpad and sometimes on the wrist rest area.

In order for the fingerprint scanner to work you need to 'enrol' your chosen finger. After you have done this, you will need to pass the finger over the scanner whenever you want to use the laptop. This acts as a sophisticated security control system as only the person with the recognised finger will be able to use the computer.

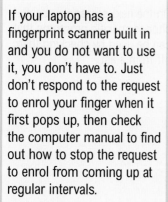

Timesaver tip

If your laptop has a fingerprint scanner built in and you do not want to use it, you don't have to. Just don't respond to the request to enrol your finger when it first pops up, then check the computer manual to find out how to stop the request to enrol from coming up at regular intervals.

Did you know?

Another practical way of protecting your details when your computer is not in use is to keep it locked away. One of the key advantages of a laptop over a desktop is that you can put it into a drawer or cupboard to hide it when it is not being used. Hiding it away like this can also prevent other people getting at it, from younger family members who you may not want to have access to your laptop, to intruders in your home.

Whatever systems you use to control access to your laptop, the device itself remains vulnerable. There are many ways in which its contents can become inaccessible. Examples include:

◼ System failure. A part of the laptop may suddenly not work, such as the hard drive failing or the screen no longer functioning.

◼ Accidental damage. It is all too easy to spill a drink over the keyboard of a laptop, rendering it unusable. People have also been known to step on laptops left on the floor, and even to drive over them. There are many ways in which a laptop can be accidentally broken.

◼ Loss or theft. People have been known to leave their laptops on public transport or in other public places by accident. Theft from the home or while out in public is also sadly experienced by some.

◼ General wear and tear. Eventually every laptop will stop working due to general wear and tear issues. Whether it is a part of the hardware or a software problem that cracks first, you should never bank on your laptop lasting for ever. Just like every other household good, it will wear out eventually.

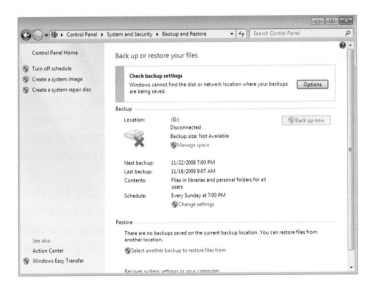

Of course everyone hopes that their laptop will not suffer unforeseen damage and that they will be in a position to replace it before it succumbs to wear and tear. But none of us can afford to be complacent about this and we should all take steps to ensure that the data stored on our laptops is backed up.

Backing up (cont.)

Fortunately, it's not difficult to do this. You just need to take a few practical and straightforward steps. Unfortunately, not enough of us back up our data well enough to be certain that the backups are completely reliable. Some people only come to the idea of backing up after they have experienced a serious loss of data. Rather than lose your family photographs, important personal documents, email history and so on, why not ensure you take good steps to back up right from the start?

It is not a good idea to put off this chore. It will probably only take a month or so for your brand new laptop to contain all sorts of data that you would really rather not lose. Having a good backup procedure in place from the start is better than putting it off for another day.

What are your options?

You have two main backup options and some 'half-way houses' at your disposal. There is no reason why you should not use both the main options together and supplement them with one or more of the half-way houses for specific projects.

There are two main backup options.

Make a complete copy of your hard drive

This is called making an 'image' of your hard drive. The process makes a precise copy of all the operating system, applications, settings and data on your computer at any one time. The idea is that if you make a complete image you can 'restore' it onto your computer if things go badly wrong.

You will need some software to do this task for you, and also a hard drive onto which to make your image. For this system to work efficiently you need to get your 'image' onto a separate hard drive. If you make it onto the internal drive of your laptop, then if the drive fails, the image will be lost too!

Make a copy of your data

As most Windows users store their documents in folders within the My Documents folder, this might at first seem like a simple matter of just copying the My Documents folder to another hard drive at regular intervals.

It is not quite as simple as this. For example, if you use Microsoft Outlook as your email, diary or contact manager, then its data is stored in a different place to the My Documents folder (you can do a search for a .pst file to find its location). Your Web browser bookmarks may also be in a different location, and some other applications may set up folders that are not inside My Documents to store the data you create with them.

The trick is to find out exactly where the data is stored by all the software you use, and then make sure you back up the contents of all these folders. You may have to do a little detective work at the start to get this right.

Available software

The good news is that there is plenty of software available that will do the task of making backups for you. You could opt for specialist backup software whose only job is to back up your data, or opt for something with a wider remit that will perform the backup function as one of many data security tasks. For an example of the latter see Norton 360 (*www.symantec.com/norton360*).

Either way, such software can make its backups at regular scheduled intervals automatically with no intervention from you once you have set up the system. And you can force a backup at any time you want to as well.

How much and how often?

People often wonder how much they should back up, and how frequently. There is no universal answer to this question, but the general rule of thumb is that more frequent backups are more useful than less frequent ones, and that if you think a piece of data on your computer is even vaguely useful it should be backed up.

We would suggest that frequent laptop users set up a daily backup, though you may find if you use your laptop less often, then weekly backups may keep your conscience happy. It is really a matter of personal taste and of what you think is appropriate. Some software will even make a backup every time

Timesaver tip

Most software lets you override its default settings for where to put backup folders. You might find changing the default setting is helpful.

8

Timesaver tip

Just as with making an 'image' it is a good idea to make backups of data to a location other than your main hard drive.

Backing up
(cont.)

you save a new version of a file if you feel you need that level of precision. The guiding principle is to back up to the degree you feel confident that you need.

To compress or not to compress?

Some backup systems can 'compress' data as they go. This can be useful if storage space is limited as files that are compressed are generally smaller than those that are not. But the downside is that you need a way of 'uncompressing' the data before you can read it. This means that if you use an external hard drive it may not be possible simply to plug it into a different computer and read data from it. You may need some additional software to help you access the backed up data.

Compressing files was thought a useful thing to do in the days when storage space was relatively expensive, but these days external hard drives of huge capacities are available at a relatively low cost.

With both of these points in mind we would advise against compressing backup data unless it is absolutely unavoidable simply because with a backup of your files uncompressed on an external hard drive, all you need to do to access them is plug the drive into any laptop you like.

External hard drives

Probably the most convenient place to send a backup is to an external hard drive. These usually plug into your laptop via a USB port, and many come with their own backup software which you can configure to your own preference.

The advantage of an external hard drive is that it is in itself portable, so you can store it away from your main computer when it is not in use for double safety.

Using an online service

Another popular option is to use an online service. These typically charge a monthly fee, and backing up is done over your Internet connection. This type of backup service is only really viable if you have broadband Internet access, because otherwise the data transfer time would be prohibitively long.

Such services use an 'incremental' system. Like software that works with an external hard drive, the first backup takes a while as it is a copy of a lot of data. Thereafter only files which are new or which have changed since last time are backed up, so the process is quicker.

Online backup services are sold on the basis that they can be fast, are automatic, and give you an 'off site' solution – which means your backup is stored somewhere away from your laptop and so is safe from the kinds of harm that could come to your laptop such as theft or being destroyed by flood or fire. They can also be accessed from any computer anywhere providing you have the necessary password.

However, online backups may not be without their own difficulties. How can you be certain that the service you have chosen to use will not suddenly be withdrawn, or that, at the precise time you need to access your backup, your Internet connection will not be down for some reason. How can you know that the data which is stored by the remote service is not going to become corrupted or in some other way made unusable?

Where to store backups

8

Where to store backups (cont.)

If you are interested in trying an online backup service, we would suggest you use it in conjunction with a more local one such as an external hard drive. As already noted, there is no harm in having two backup systems, and there may be times when the remote backup is precisely what you need, and other times when the local one is perfect for your requirements.

Half-way houses and extra backups

There is a variety of options for making short-term or partial backups, or making backups of specific types of file which can double as permanent storage for multiple users.

Here are some examples:

- Create CDs. This is a good option for photographs, for example. You could create photo CDs by theme, by year, to remember particular holidays or occasions or using some other criteria. You can store these somewhere away from your computer for easy access. Not only do they provide an extra backup in addition to your main system, they are very handy when you want to remind yourself of last year's family holiday or show friends a group of photos on a particular theme, for example.

- Use a USB flash drive. This is a good option if you are working on a particular project and like to carry the files that relate to it with you and know they are secure. An example might be if you are writing a long and complex document. All the time it was being written a copy of this book was kept on a USB flash drive so that it could be worked on easily using different computers. It was a mix of a backup and a working tool.

Important points to remember about backing up data

- Check your backups from time to time to make sure the 'medium' you are using remains intact and is not itself corrupted.

- Do it regularly. There is no point in setting up a system, such as an external hard drive, onto which you want to copy all of your data, making that copy, and then forgetting about it. Every time you create a new file, copy a photograph to your laptop from your camera, or whatever, you need to be sure it is going to be backed up. The easiest way to do this is to look for software that can do its backup automatically at set intervals, or even make its backup whenever you edit a document or create a new one.

- Store your backups somewhere safe. If you are going on holiday and use an external hard drive, why not ask a neighbour to care for it on your behalf.

- Have more than one system if you feel more comfortable and confident this way.

- Do not back up to your laptop's hard drive. If the hard drive fails and becomes inaccessible, the backup is inaccessible too. Whatever system(s) you choose, make sure they are external to your computer.

Where to store backups (cont.)

8

Laptop security II: the Internet

Introduction

If you intend to use the Internet at all – and it is almost certain that you will want to do this – then you need to consider very seriously how to protect your computer from all manner of problems that using the Internet is associated with. As almost all of us with computers use the Internet, most often for email and Web browsing, security is a very important issue to address.

> **Important**
>
> Do not go onto the Internet until you are absolutely certain you have adequately protected your laptop against intruders.

!

How to keep intruders out

What should you worry about?

Malicious software and emails with malicious content, attachments or weblinks are a serious threat to your enjoyment of computing. You should do all you can to avoid them. If you start to research this topic on the Internet you are likely to come across a lot of different terms and it can be very confusing at first. With that in mind, we describe some of the most common terms you will encounter (see the Jargon buster box).

Jargon buster

Viruses: computer programs that get onto your computer without your knowledge and can then reproduce without you ever knowing. Viruses can spread between computers via the Internet or can get onto a computer from a CD, USB drive or other 'infected' medium. Viruses need not be harmful to your computer, though many are. Not to be confused with 'malware' which describes more malicious software.

Malware: a collective name for a whole group of software which can get onto your computer without your knowledge in similar ways to a virus. Malware includes software such as key loggers, spyware and adware.

Spyware: software that is installed without your knowledge and can then perform various activities without your consent. This includes monitoring your computing activities to collect personal information and directing your Web browser to selected websites that may themselves contain further undesirable software which could automatically install itself onto your computer.

Adware: this is not always unwanted. Some software is free to download and use, and is supported by advertising. It is known as adware, and if you choose to accept the advertising element, then you are clearly OK about having it on your computer. However, some types of adware can be classed as malware as they get onto your computer surreptitiously rather than being sanctioned by you. These can cause advertising to pop up at unwanted intervals, perhaps when you are using the Internet, perhaps not.

Jargon buster

Key logger: software which monitors which key presses you make and sends the information to a recipient via the Internet without your knowledge. This is potentially very powerful information and can cause you considerable problems. From what you type over a period of time it is possible to learn the email addresses of your online bank(s) and your password(s), logins for any secure websites you use, and any other information you care to type. With enough information it is possible to log into your bank account and transfer money, make online purchases using your login details for websites and credit card information, and conduct various other online activities using your identity.

Phishing: this starts with email. You are sent an email containing a website address you need to go to in order to complete the action it advises. The website will not be an official one but a fake, and it might send the information you enter into it, such as bank details or passwords, to a fraudster. Banks and other financial institutions are notoriously associated with phishing emails, but the practice extends into other areas too.

Who are these intruders?

First, we need to make it clear that it is not difficult to keep intruders out of your laptop. There are some steps you need to take, but none is daunting or requires copious amounts of technical knowledge. The most important thing about this section is that you read and understand it, and that you take the recommended action.

The first thing to understand is what we mean by intruders. There are several types of intruder to consider:

- Any person, known to you or not, who is in physical proximity to your computer and who you don't want to get access to your computer and/or the files on it. Such a person could be a family member, friend or housemate for

9

How to keep intruders out (cont.)

example. We have covered this in Chapter 8 when we talked about setting up passwords.

- People using your Internet connection account without your authorisation. Strictly speaking these people are not accessing your computer. Rather, they are accessing your wireless modem – which is what you use to get onto the Internet. In doing this they are using a computer-related resource which belongs to you and whose management and care are your responsibility. We will discuss this later in this chapter.

- People gaining access to important information you store on your computer via automated agents that gather information and return it to them. Broadly these people are using what is termed 'malware'.

- Automated intruders which are produced by people but don't return any information to them. Broadly these are what are known as computer viruses. These can cause damage to your computer in many ways, and at their worst can delete files and even corrupt your entire hard drive. We will discuss dealing with automated intruders and automated agents below.

How might these unwanted elements (we'll call them intruders) get onto your computer? There are various different methods.

Via media like CDs or USB keydrives

One possibility is that intruders might gain access if you install software or other files onto your laptop that are passed to you by someone else on a CD, DVD or other medium. It is possible for software in addition to that which you know you are installing to be installed without your knowledge at the time. To protect against this you need to be sure you have adequate anti-virus and anti-malware software installed (see below).

Another possibility is that intruders may gain access if you download software or other files from the Internet and then install them. The same situation applies here as with software given to you on CD, DVD or another medium, and the same preventative measures apply too.

Via websites

Intruders may also get access to your computer via the Internet when you browse websites. In these circumstances often you don't even need to choose to do any downloading at all. Malicious and hidden software coding in the websites in question can do the job of installing undesired software discretely and without your knowledge.

Via instant messaging software

You should also be wary of intruders using instant messaging software to get onto your computer. While many see instant messaging (usually abbreviated to IM) as simply another way to contact friends or work colleagues to chat to online in real time and share files, it is increasingly used as a way to distribute malware.

The problem generally comes with the file sharing aspect of IM services. Just to be on the safe side you should never click a link or try to download a file if you aren't confident of the source. And even if a file or link seems to come from someone you know, it could have been sent without their knowledge, so make sure you are confident the sender really did send the file or link and does want you to have it before you click.

How viruses and malware get onto your computer

Timesaver tip

When downloading software always be aware that malware can be incorporated within it. Try to check that your software source is legitimate and not likely to carry software you don't know about.

Timesaver tip

If your laptop is for family use insist that younger users don't download anything without asking you first. Younger users may not be aware of the potential pitfalls of downloading software with malware attached to it.

9

How viruses and malware get onto your computer (cont.)

Via email

And then there is email. Your Internet Service Provider (ISP) may have software which blocks some email, and software which you install on your computer is designed to alert you to and block other software. But inevitably some malicious email will get through. Your job is to be on the lookout for it and when you find it take appropriate action.

Malicious emails can have attachments which you click on to launch the fraudulent software or take you to a fraudulent website, can ask for you to respond by email with requested information, or can have software buried within them so that just reading them can be enough to initiate an attack.

Timesaver tip

Check your email software for a setting that allows you to turn off HTML in the preview view. Viewing email as HTML means you can see visually rich messages with graphics and colour implemented, but it also means that some software embedded in emails can run automatically. Turning off the HTML in preview mode lets you view an email before opening it, but disables the HTML which may contain malicious code.

Examples of malicious email and email scams

In every case if you are unsure of an email bearing these characteristics, you should delete it immediately without looking at it.

- Emails suggesting they contain images you may be drawn to and offering a link to see them. Do *not* click the link as it will almost certainly take you to a suspect website, which could attempt to download unwanted software onto your computer.

- Emails purporting to be from your bank, building society or other financial institution asking for some sort of account verification. Financial institutions never send emails asking for this type of information. The same goes for emails from a website you make purchases from or which for some other reason has some personal information about you.

Timesaver tip

The appropriate action in any case where you are concerned about an email is always to delete it without opening it and preferably off your system completely.

- Emails which ask you for any kind of password or other 'secret' information. No organisation which takes its online security seriously would ask you to verify this type of information by email.

- Emails asking for information which suggest you should act immediately, even including a phrase suggesting account suspension or other serious action if you don't reply quickly. These are often fraudulent.

- Emails which purport to come from official sources but which incorporate spelling errors or poor English.

- Emails that alert you to a virus or spoof and direct you to a website, or suggest a download or have an attachment to deal with the problem. No legitimate organisation working with viruses or other malicious content would ever send out individual email alerts and fixes unless you have specifically chosen to receive them, usually by subscribing to an email service.

Timesaver tip

Set your anti-virus software to check incoming email as it arrives. This may slightly slow down your computer but the speed difference is unlikely to be appreciable and it should mean any email that potentially has viruses attached will be flagged for your attention immediately.

Email is not the only way that viruses can get into your computer. They can also come from infected files you open from external media. So set your anti-virus software to check all files as they are opened. This includes files opened as email attachments and those opened from external media such as USB flash drives.

How viruses and malware get onto your computer (cont.)

9

How viruses and malware get onto your computer (cont.)

Protecting your computer

If this all sounds rather daunting, don't be too put off. There are some straightforward steps you can take to protect your computer. The trick is to actually take the steps, set up the right systems on your computer, and make sure everything you have set up is always up to date and running effectively.

You should do all three things we discuss below before even thinking about starting to use the Internet seriously. Even a few minutes of unprotected Internet access can leave your laptop vulnerable to attacks. The three things are:

- make sure your operating system security settings are configured correctly
- ensure you have appropriate security software installed
- protect your network.

Check the security options that your operating system offers. If you want to use them, make sure they are switched on. If you would prefer to use alternatives, you can switch them off.

In Windows 7, XP and Vista you will find the security settings in the Security Centre, located in the Windows Control Panel. The options available will be as follows.

Windows Firewall

A firewall is a piece of software which monitors connections to and from the Internet. If software on your computer tries to access the Internet, or a connection is attempted from the Internet, the firewall will spot it. If you designate connections as allowed then they are let through, but if you designate them as not allowed they will be blocked.

A firewall doesn't keep asking you every time a connection is made to or from the Internet. It remembers what is and is not allowed. So it might spot an Internet connection attempt from a newly installed piece of software the first time it is attempted and ask you if the connection is to be allowed. If you say 'yes' this is remembered for subsequent connections.

Some people say that if your modem/router has a firewall then you don't need one running on your laptop as well. We would disagree. Certainly, all the time you are using your own modem/router, with a set-up you should understand and an enabled firewall, then having one on your laptop might seem like overkill.

But you have chosen a laptop rather than a desktop PC because it is portable, and so it is likely you will carry it around at least some of the time. Imagine, for example, that you take your laptop out of your home and use it on a free public Wi-Fi network to access the Internet. How do you know that the firewall systems in operation are reliable and trustworthy? And what about when you take your laptop to a friend's house. Are you prepared to ask if their router firewall is switched on? And what will you do if they say that they don't really understand all that stuff? Far better to take responsibility yourself and have a firewall running on your laptop for those occasions.

Operating system security settings

Timesaver tip

Make sure you set your security software to run at all times. This should be automatic, but familiarise yourself with how the software works to ensure you have made the setting.

Timesaver tip

Don't just automatically say 'yes' to every connection attempt your firewall alerts you to. Make a point of understanding what is being asked for. One day, one of those attempts will be something you don't want to happen, and an automatic 'yes' could lead to disaster.

9

Operating system security settings (cont

If you really don't want to have both modem/router and laptop firewalls running simultaneously, you can turn the laptop one off when you are somewhere you know is already protected, and turn it on when you go into an area you are not sure about.

Turn on the Windows Firewall in Windows 7

1 Click Start and choose the Control Panel.

2 Choose System and Security.

3 Choose Windows Firewall.

4 In the left-hand window choose Turn Windows Firewall on or off.

5 You can now choose when to use the Firewall.

Timesaver tip

If you don't already know, now is the time to check your modem/router and reassure yourself that its firewall is turned on.

Did you know?

You can use features built into Windows Vista to help ensure your computer is protected against intrusions. The Windows Vista Security Centre provides access to built-in and third-party security software.

Windows Defender

This is anti-spyware software that comes with Windows Vista and Windows 7. You can download it from Microsoft's website for Windows XP. Note that Windows Defender is not anti-virus software, so if you want to use it you will need third-party anti-virus software as well. There are also many third-party anti-spyware options.

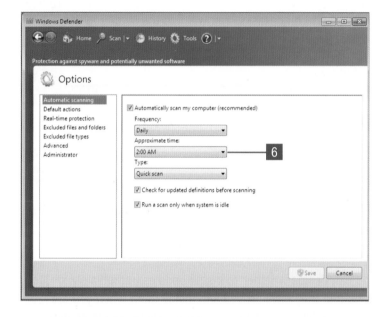

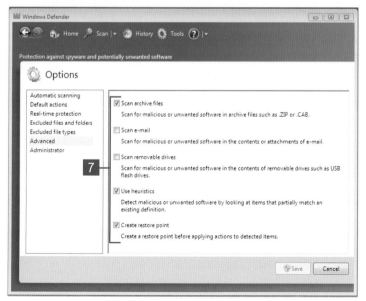

Set up Windows Defender in Windows 7

1 Click Start and in the search box type Windows Defender.

2 Click Windows Defender from the list.

3 If you are prompted to turn on Windows Defender then do so unless you have already installed an alternative anti-spyware application.

4 Choose Tools from the menu at the top of the screen.

5 Choose Options.

6 Now you can decide how you want Windows Defender to run. Setting an automatic scan at a scheduled time is the best option. Choose the time that suits you.

7 Check the options in the right-hand column and make any additional settings you feel necessary. For example, under Advanced you may want to get Defender to scan all the alternative sources listed including external hard drives and email.

9

Operating system security settings (cont.)

Automatic updating

Microsoft updates its operating system quite frequently, and many of these updates are to do with improving its security while others increase the reliability of the software.

The updates are sent over the Internet to registered users. If you set up your laptop for automatic updating these updates will be received automatically, downloading over the Internet while you do other tasks. You will find the setting in the Control Panel.

Timesaver tip

Your anti-virus software and anti-spyware software should be able to update itself automatically whenever you go onto the Internet. Make sure that this setting is enabled. That way you won't need to remember to keep it aware of all the latest threats, as this will happen without your intervention. You will find that your software is likely to update itself as frequently as daily.

For your information

You can choose between asking Windows to install updates automatically or let you set your own schedule for when these updates are downloaded and installed.

You can decide whether to install updates immediately, or just to be told they have arrived and install them when you are ready. The latter is a better choice for some people as the installation process can require you to reboot your computer, and this can be inconvenient to do if you are in the middle of another task.

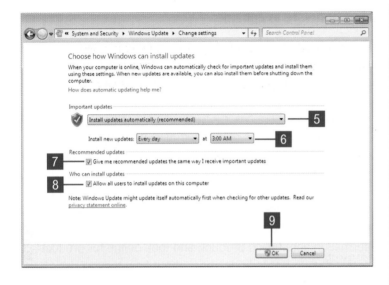

Configure Windows Update in Windows 7

1 Click Start and choose the Control Panel.

2 Choose System and Security.

3 Choose Windows Update.

4 In the left-hand column choose Change Settings.

5 Click the arrow under Important updates and decide how you want to install them.

6 Decide when you want to install the updates. If the computer is switched off at the chosen time, updates will be installed the next time it is switched on.

7 You can decide to accept recommended as well as important updates in the same way.

8 You can allow any user to install updates.

9 When you are finished click OK.

9

Operating system security settings (cont.)

Timesaver tip

Your anti-virus and anti-spyware software may be able to be scheduled to 'sweep' your computer at regular intervals. Even if you have ongoing checking of new files downloaded and opened, a regular full check is a good idea. You can set this to run at a regular interval, say once a week, at a time when you are not normally using your computer.

Some software to consider

We can't cover all the possible available software here, but the table on page 224 shows some of the more widely used software for protecting your laptop against viruses, spyware and intrusions.

Some of the companies mentioned have more than one product, but we have selected just one from each company.

Some of the software listed performs a single task, others perform several tasks. We have listed some of the key tasks performed, but you should check the websites for more information about each product, and look online for product reviews if you want to know more about how they work.

9

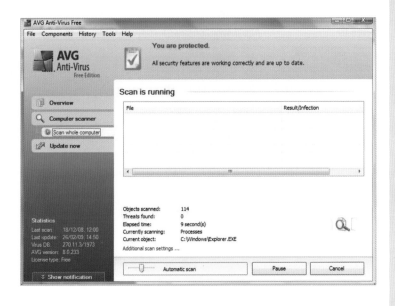

Operating system security settings (cont.)

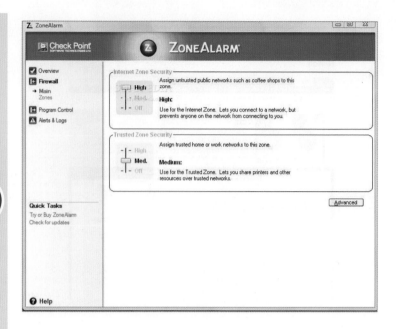

For your information

One example of firewall software is Zone Alarm. In this picture you can see settings being made for the level of security that should apply to your laptop.

		Price *	Website
Zone Alarm from Check Point	√ Firewall X Virus X Spyware	Free to non-commercial users	*http://www.zonealarm.com*
Internet Security Suite from McAfee	√ Firewall √ Virus √ Spyware Some additional features: Email spam prevention Identity theft protection	Software is charged for	*http://uk.mcafee.com*
Norton 360 from Symantec	√ Firewall √ Virus √ Spyware Some additional features: Email spam prevention Identity theft protection Phishing protection	Software is charged for	*http://www.symantec.com*
SpySweeper from Webroot	X Firewall X Virus √ Spyware	Software is charged for	*http://www.webroot.co.uk*

		Price *	Website
Panda Internet Security 2008 from Panda	√ Firewall √ Virus √ Spyware Some additional features: Email spam prevention Identity theft protection Phishing protection	Software is charged for	http://www.pandasecurity.com/uk
AVG Anti-Virus	X Firewall √ Virus X Spyware	Free for home and non-commercial use	http://free.avg.com
Avast! Antivirus	X Firewall √ Virus X Spyware	Free for home and non-commercial use	http://www.avast.com
Comodo	√ Firewall X Virus X Spyware	Free	http://www.personalfirewall.comodo.com
Ad-Aware	X Firewall X Virus √ Spyware	Free for home and non-commercial use	http://www.lavasoft.com
Spybot Search and Destroy	X Firewall X Virus √ Spyware	Free for home and non-commercial use	http://www.safer-networking.org
Spyware Blaster	X Firewall X Virus √ Spyware	Free for personal and non-commercial use	http://www.javacoolsoftware.com

9

* Software noted as free may be free to home users provided they are not involved in any kind of commercial activity with their computer. The software may also be free to users involved in education. If you are interested in a piece of software that is noted as being free to some users, you should read the terms and conditions on the website carefully. Even if software is designated as free for you to use, you may be able to make a donation. Doing so can help software developers continue to work on their software and develop it into the future, so making a donation is generally a good idea.

Operating system security settings (cont.)

Timesaver tip

Ensure your anti-virus and anti-malware software is set to automatic updating wherever this is supported. That way it will keep itself up to date with new information about the latest threats without your intervention.

Charges

Where you are charged a fee for security software there are usually two elements.

The initial charge will be for the software itself and for a period of updates to the reference database it uses. Typically this lasts for a year. The software will monitor the date and tell you as the end of this period approaches. Then in good time you will be asked to pay a fee to renew your subscription to the software for a further period – typically this will again be a year though there may be discounts if you extend for a longer period.

Alerting you to problems

Anti-virus and anti-malware software uses its own database of information about the software it is guarding against. It checks this against what is on your computer, and against incoming email and downloads for example, and where it finds a problem it alerts you.

You can then 'quarantine' the suspect item, and delete it from your computer before it has had the chance to do any damage.

Clearly for the software to do its job efficiently it needs to have an up-to-date database of information to work from. New viruses and malware appear very frequently, so it is extremely important that the databases used by your software are kept up to date.

Much anti-virus and anti-malware software has an automatic updating system that uses your broadband Internet connection to keep itself updated. You need to make sure this is switched on, and then check periodically that it remains switched on. Some freeware uses manual updating systems though, and here it will be your responsibility to make sure you keep it up to date. Setting yourself regular diary reminders should do the trick.

The steps we have covered above concentrate on ensuring that your laptop itself is protected against intrusions of all kinds. It is important to ensure that access to your wireless network and wireless Internet connection is also protected. This is important even if you have only one computer.

Multi-computer households

Many households have more than one computer. In these circumstances they may use their wireless modem/router to allow them to share access to the Internet. They may even set up an arrangement in which one computer acts as a 'server' or a central hub containing some files that other computers can share. Examples of such files might include music or photographs.

In these circumstances, each computer can connect to the Internet via a single modem attached to your telephone line. The computers could connect to the modem by a physical wire (called Ethernet), or by a system that uses the electricity plugs in your home (called power line).

The most frequently used way of computers connecting to the Internet, though, is to use Wi-Fi (see Chapter 4 for more on Wi-Fi). Each computer you want to connect in this way must have Wi-Fi either built in or added via a peripheral, and the modem/router must have it too.

Single computer households

In households with one computer Wi-Fi may still be the preferred way to connect to the Internet. Using a wired (Ethernet) connection means that a physical link needs to be made between the computer and modem. A power line solution is more flexible, but you still need to be near a mains power socket to use an Internet connection.

Wi-Fi allows greater freedom in that all you need to do is be in range of the Wi-Fi signal to get a connection. Theoretically this means you could access the Internet from any room in your home or from your garden if you have one.

9

Protect your network (cont.)

Because Wi-Fi means you can access the Internet in this untethered way, it also means other people could use your Internet connection too. Without some sort of protection set up any computer within Wi-Fi range can use your Internet connection.

Having unauthorised people use your Internet connection could cause you some difficulties. If you have a broadband service with a cap on the amount of data you are able to download each month, any unauthorised use could push you over the cap, thereby costing you additional money.

It is also possible that an unauthorised person could use your Internet connection for purposes you disapprove of or are even illegal.

The way to protect against such intrusions is to set up the security systems that are built into your ADSL router.

Routers from different manufacturers function differently, and so for the detail on how to set up security systems you will need to consult your router manual. However, we now explain things you can do to help ensure your wireless Internet access is secure from unwanted users.

Router passwords

Router settings are usually managed via your Web browser. You type a numerical address into your browser, and then enter a password and user name in order to get to the settings area.

Typically the password and user name will be set to a default setting by the manufacturer. It is important to change them. The default settings and the numerical address for your Web browser are widely known, and if you don't change the user name and password anybody could come along and start toying with your router settings. At worst they could gain access to your secure group of users or even lock you out of your own router and Internet network completely.

Set up WEP or WPA encryption

Your router can be set to encode information it sends so that it is difficult to read if it is intercepted. There are several different standards, and the two you are most likely to come across are referred to as WEP and WPA. Of the two WPA is the 'stronger' and therefore the better choice.

But note that whatever standard you choose *must* be shared by all the devices on your system. Some older devices might not support the more advanced WPA standard, so check the capabilities of every device before you set up encryption.

Consider using fixed IP addresses

Every device that connects to your router has an 'address' which allows the device to be identified. You can allow your network to assign these addresses automatically using a system called DHCP. Many computer users like this system as it allows computers to slot into their network easily.

Setting up security on your router

9

Setting up security on your router (cont.)

However, you might find it more useful to use a system called 'static IP addresses'. Here you assign an address to each computer you want to be allowed onto your network, then tell the router what addresses it is allowed to connect to. Your router manual will explain how to do this in more detail.

Turn on your router firewall

Even if you have a firewall on your laptop, you should also turn on the firewall on your router. In fact, having both running at the same time offers you increased protection against intrusions from external computers.

Change the default SSID

You can think of the SSID as the name of your router. All routers have one, and one is set by default by the manufacturer. Changing it won't do anything to improve computer security, but it might indicate to a 'driveby' hacker that your system is likely to be secure. After all, if you go to all the trouble of changing your router's name you are likely to have made other, more significant, security settings. Whatever you choose for your new name, avoid things like your address, name or any other personal information.

Low-tech ideas can be useful as well as high-tech ones and we have two to suggest.

Switch off when not in use

Not only will switching off your router when it is not in use save energy – which means both reducing your unnecessary energy usage and saving money – it will also reduce the chances of your system being hacked into.

You could turn the router off when you go to bed at night, and when you are away from home, for example, as well as at times when you know you will not be using the Internet for extended periods. If you do find you need the Internet, it should take less than a minute for your system to be back up and running when you switch it back on.

Position your router centrally within the home

The range of a wireless signal varies but it can be quite extensive. To help keep as much of the signal within your home as possible try to position your router in a central location in your home rather than by an external wall. Doing this could mean that the signal strength outside your home is too weak for another computer to easily access it.

Find the optimum location for your router

1 Work out where you are most likely to want to use the Internet most often.

2 Consider the construction of your home. Are there thick walls? Is it on more than two levels?

3 Try to position your router where it has the least interrupted line of sight to the place you are most likely to want to use the Internet from.

4 Take into consideration that routers work best when they are directly connected to the primary phone socket.

9

5 Try moving the router around a little to see if you can get the signal to stretch further if you have it in different locations.

Passwords

At this point it is worth making a generic note about passwords. In the wider world the advice is not to write down passwords and other data such as PIN numbers. However, there is a view that for computers and Internet use it is actually a good idea to write down passwords and then store them somewhere very safe.

'Somewhere safe' means *not* on your mobile phone, and *not* in your computer contact management software where they are easily identified with what they control access to.

One alternative is to write passwords on paper and store them somewhere very safe. Another is to use software to store all passwords in one place and then control access to all of them with a single password. You may feel a system like this is more secure than using paper. Such software can often synchronise software on your laptop with software on a smartphone if you carry one, so that your passwords are with you at all times but are themselves protected by an overarching password. If you like this idea you need to ensure your smartphone has very good security of its own and be ready to change all your passwords if you lose your smartphone.

Why record passwords?

There are two main reasons. First of all, you are likely to set up a lot of passwords during your time as a computer user. For your wireless router, for email accounts, for banking accounts, for websites, and more. Ideally you should use different passwords each time, and should change passwords frequently. Then if someone discovers one password, they won't be able to access all your passworded accounts.

Passwords should be a mix of letters and numbers, and not things that are easy to guess like your name or house number. However, if you follow these principles you may find it difficult to remember your passwords! Writing them down and storing them somewhere very secure is a failsafe system.

Secondly, in the unfortunate circumstance that you become unable to use your laptop for some reason, you may want to ask a trusted person to do some tasks for you. They may well need access to your passwords to do this. In such circumstances giving them access to all your passwords in one place could be the most useful thing for both of you.

Optimising your laptop

Introduction

Your laptop is a complex piece of equipment and you need to use it with care to make sure you get the best out of it. Other chapters in this book look at this topic from the angles of security (Chapters 8 and 9) and taking general care of your laptop (Chapter 5).

In this chapter we want to look at some of the more techno-savvy things you can do to ensure that the internal parts of your laptop remain in tip-top condition and it functions smoothly and efficiently.

From the very first time you install your first piece of software onto a new laptop you are moving away from its pristine 'fresh out of the box' state. You'll certainly be adding to the amount of information stored on its hard drive. You may also be making subtle changes you don't even notice you are making.

Why are changes like these of any significance? Because they can all make a difference to how your computer works. Small individual changes might not have a noticeable effect. But over time the cumulative effect of the changes could cause your computer to run slowly and even, eventually, to stop running at all.

So in this chapter we are going to look at various ways of keeping your computer in tip-top condition and functioning as you want it to.

What you'll do

Changing file associations

Saving files in a particular format

Software that runs automatically

The Windows Registry

Battery and power management

Optimising your hard drive

Regular reboots

Changing file associations

A file association is a very straightforward thing to understand. All file names are made up of two parts. Examples might be

- mynovel.doc
- budget.xls
- leaflet.pdf
- song.mp3

The part to the left of the dot is the description for each file. This is assigned by you and is designed to help you find a document when you search for it.

The part to the right of the dot is called the 'file extension', and it describes the file type. So, in our examples above, mynovel.doc is a Microsoft Word file, budget.xls is a Microsoft Excel file, leaflet.pdf is a PDF file, and song.mp3 is a music file in the MP3 format.

Now, think of file extensions in a slightly different way. They can be automatically linked to software so that when you double-click a file it opens in the appropriate application. This is called a 'file association'.

You might have several bits of software on your computer that can open files of certain types. For example, a music player can usually recognise music files of several different types, and you could easily have two or more different music players on your laptop.

When you install a piece of software it might ask you what file types to associate with it. You can select these manually. But you may install software that changes one or more file associations without asking you first.

So, what you can easily end up with is a file that, when double-clicked, doesn't open in the software you would prefer it to. This can be at best confusing and irritating, but at worst it can reduce your productivity since you may be familiar with using another piece of software to work on your file and not want to get to know a new one.

The good news is that you can manually change the file associations and it is very easy to do. Changing the setting for one file will automatically change the setting for all other files that share its extension.

In Windows 7:

- open the Control Panel
- choose Programs
- under Default Programs choose 'Make a file type always open in a specific program'
- scroll through to find the file extension you want
- click the extension by highlighting it, then click Choose Program
- click the program you want to use
- click OK.

In Windows Vista:

- open the Control Panel
- choose Default Programs and now you have two options:
  - choose Default Programs, select a program and then either: choose to 'set this program as default' which means letting it open all the file types it is associated with; or choose 'choose defaults for this program' which means you get to choose which file types it is associated with
  - choose 'associate a file type or protocol with a program'
- scroll through to find the file extension you want
- click the extension to highlight it then click Change Program
- if the software you want is not listed click Browse and find the program you want, select it, then click OK.

In Windows XP:

- view the file in Windows Explorer
- right-click the file
- choose Open With and select Choose Program
- select the program you want from the list
- make sure 'Always use the selected program to open this kind of file' is ticked
- click OK.

Changing file associations (cont.)

Did you know?

You can choose which programs are used to open particular files when you click on them.

10

Saving files in a particular format

Much software lets you save files in one of a number of different formats. This can be very useful if you want to use one piece of software to create a file and another piece of software to open it. For example, you might prefer one word processor but know that the person to whom you are sending a file prefers another, which may not be able to open the type of file your software automatically creates.

To save as a different file format, you can usually choose 'Save As' from the File menu, then choose 'Save as type' to pick your file type.

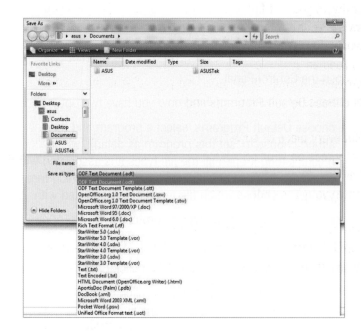

When you switch on your laptop a lot of software runs automatically. This can be a real boon. If, for example, you are a fan of podcasts and you like to keep up to date with your favourites, a podcast downloader can be set to run automatically whenever your computer is turned on. It will scan for updates to your favourite podcasts, and download them automatically. Then when you are ready to listen you can either do so directly on your laptop or copy the podcasts to a portable music player.

To take a different type of example, when you install anti-virus software you will find that it runs automatically when you switch your computer on. This is great because it is there working as soon as you start using your computer. It is ready to keep an eye on everything you do, and alert you to any problems it finds. It can also use your Internet connection to automatically download updates.

But every piece of software that runs automatically uses up resources on your computer, in particular system memory, and having lots of software running in the background can slow down your computer considerably.

The goal, then, is to have a minimal number of applications running automatically so that you can maximise the resources available for the software you are actually using.

Software that runs automatically

Important

When you view a list of startup programs you may see a lot of items listed. You may find that you don't recognise many of them. Some are vital for Windows and must not be removed. So you should take care only to delete items you are certain are not a central element of Windows. Deleting something vital for Windows could mean your computer will not boot the next time you want to use it. Proceed with caution!

10

Software that runs automatically (cont.)

In Windows 7 you can see a list of some of the software that runs at startup by clicking Start, choosing Programs and then choosing Startup. You can drag applications in and out of this folder depending on whether you want them to run automatically when you switch on your laptop.

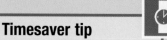

Timesaver tip

In the interests of keeping your computer running as smoothly as possible it is good practice to close any applications you are not currently using.

The Windows Registry is a complex and vital part of your computer. It is a store for settings for the operating system, hardware, software, user preferences and so on. It also stores information which is used deeper within the operating system. It is referred to by the operating system for information it contains and if it becomes damaged in any way it can cause your computer to work incorrectly or fail to start up.

Nobody should attempt to change anything in the registry unless they feel very confident about what they are doing. There are tools and utilities you can use to edit the contents of the registry, but we would not suggest trying them unless you are very confident about what you are doing.

Because this book is aimed at newcomers to computing we are going to leave it at that. If you feel there is something wrong with your computer's registry, we suggest you find a computer consultant to take a look rather than trying to tackle the problem yourself.

The Windows Registry

10

Battery and power management

If you have chosen to buy a laptop rather than a desktop the chances are that a key reason for your choice is the ability it offers for you to work in different locations and away from mains power.

The battery is the vital component here. You will know what the manufacturer's estimated battery life is for your computer. In the real world this can vary enormously depending on the strain you put on your computer. For example, if you are a keen user of wireless networking over Wi-Fi you may find that the battery drains more quickly than you might expect, simply because the Wi-Fi hardware requires more battery power to keep it operational.

There are several steps you can take to conserve battery power.

- Close applications that you do not need. Even if they are just open and sitting in the background not being used, applications consume battery power. It might not amount to a lot, but it is worth conserving every trickle that might drain from the battery.

- Turn down the screen brightness. You may not need to have the screen at its full brightness level all the time when working on battery power. Experiment with the screen brightness controls. You should be able to find a brightness level that is below the brightest and comfortable for your eyes.

- Use the power settings. Regardless of your operating system your laptop should have some power scheme settings. These can be configured for various power saving activities. You can implement separate settings for when you are working on battery and on mains power.

- Eco mode. Some laptops have an 'eco mode' setting. You may find a button near the keyboard which sets this running. It might do things like turn off some ports, adjust the screen setting or reduce power to the optical drive in order to conserve battery power.

The hard drive of your computer is the storage centre for all your data and applications. It is important that you keep it in good condition. For the most part the hard drive works perfectly well unattended, but from time to time you might want to consider 'optimising' or 'defragmenting' it.

Here's why. When a file is saved onto your hard drive it is not saved all in one place. Instead it is broken up into small chunks and each chunk is put onto the hard drive The parts are known as 'fragments'. When you want to open the file again the computer has to reassemble all the fragments back into the file.

As your hard drive has more and more data saved onto it, the fragments can be separated further and further apart and so can take longer to pull back together again.

You can get over this problem by using the defragmenter tool that comes with Windows, or by using a third-party tool if you prefer.

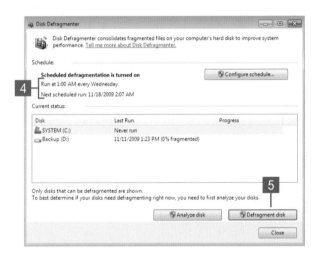

Did you know?

If your laptop is new and has little data on it you probably won't see much benefit from defragmenting your hard drive. But as you amass more and more data, defragmenting every few months can be a good discipline. It might not make your computer run like the wind, but it could lead to an improvement in performance.

Optimising your hard drive

Optimise your hard drive in Windows 7

1 Click Start and choose the Control Panel.

2 Choose System and Security.

3 Under Administration Tools choose Defragment your Hard Drive.

4 Decide whether you want this process to happen at regular intervals and create a schedule if you do.

5 Click Defragment disk if you want the process to begin immediately.

10

Regular reboots

As you add and run more applications they consume more of your laptop's RAM memory. This can cause your system to run slowly. Some applications can even continue to consume memory after you have closed them. The best solution to having an optimal amount of free memory in your computer is to switch it off and on at regular intervals.

We would certainly suggest that you switch off your computer when it is not in use, both to keep the memory usage under control and to reduce power consumption. You will be paying for the energy used to keep an unused laptop switched on, and using energy that you don't need to.

Appendix: major laptop brands and their websites

Below is a list of the major laptop brands and their websites. If you have access to the Internet you can use this list to find out about laptops currently available in the UK before buying them.

Acer: *www.acer.co.uk*

Alienware: *www.Alienware.co.uk*

Apple: *www.apple.com/uk*

Asus: *www.asus.com*

Dell: *www.dell.co.uk*

Fujitsu: *www.fujitsu.com/uk*

Gateway: *www.uk.gateway.com*

Hewlett-Packard: *www.hp.com/uk*

Hi-Grade: *www.higrade.com*

Lenovo: *www.lenovo.com/uk*

MSI: *www.msicomputer.co.uk*

Novatech: *http://www.novatech.co.uk*

Panasonic: *www.toughbook-europe.com*

Samsung: *www.samsung.com/uk*

Sony: *www.sonystyle.co.uk*

Toshiba: *www.toshiba.co.uk*

Zepto: *www.zepto.com*

Jargon buster

802.11 – The name given to a wireless communications standard widely used for wireless networking. Also known as Wi-Fi.

ADSL – Asymmetric Digital Subscriber Line. The technology you use to connect to the Internet. You do this via a modem which is connected to your phone line and your computer. People often use the term broadband instead of ADSL.

Blog – A website you can produce to present your thoughts on a particular topic. Some people refer to blogs as online diaries, but they can be much more than this, covering anything from hobbies to political campaigns.

Bluetooth – A wireless technology designed typically to connect just two devices together for a short period of time, and over a short distance: for example, a mobile phone and a wireless headset or a laptop computer and a mobile phone or smartphone.

Broadband – The term used to describe modern high speed Internet connections.

Card reader – A device for accessing flash memory cards such as SD, microSD, Memory Stick and xD picture cards. These are built into many laptops and can also be added as a peripheral.

CPU – Central Processor Unit. Also known simply as the processor. The part of a computer that runs applications. Several companies make processors for computers, including Intel and AMD.

Desktop computer – The term used to describe computers designed to stay in one location. Typically there are several separate components. A 'case' houses the hard drive, processor and other key components. The screen, keyboard and mouse are attached by cables instead of being integrated as they are in a laptop.

Desktop replacement – A generic term for a laptop designed primarily to sit on a desk and not be moved about much. Tends to have a large screen and be heavy.

Docking station – An add-on for your laptop that gives it a wider range of ports and connectors than are built into it. These can be useful if you want to connect lots of hardware when your laptop is on your desk.

Ethernet – A system for connecting devices such as two computers by wires. Laptops have Ethernet capability and a connection socket built into them.

ExpressCard – A type of connector. Used to connect peripherals to a laptop.

Firewall – Software on your laptop that helps prevent unauthorised access. A firewall is vital if you are an Internet user.

Firewire – A type of connector. Used to connect peripherals to a laptop.

Hard drive – The storage area of your computer. The hard drive is where all the documents and other materials you produce are stored, where all the applications you install are stored, and where the operating system is stored.

HDMI – High Definition Multimedia Interface. A type of connector. Used to send digital video from your laptop to a TV or other device.

HSDPA – High Speed Downlink Packet Access. A data download technology used by 3G mobile phone networks. Currently top download speeds available are 7.2 Mbps in a very few areas and 3.6 Mbps more widely. In the future connection speeds are expected to rise to 14.4 Mbps. Data connection speeds depend on services provided by your network operator.

LAN – Local Area Network. A LAN allows you to connect one or more devices together in order that they can share information with each other, such as joining two computers together so they can share data.

Laptop computer – An alternative term for a notebook or portable computer.

Linux – An 'open source' operating system. Open source software is free and is maintained by a broad based user community. Linux is available in several 'packages' known as 'distributions' and you may be charged a small handling and mailing fee if you choose one of these. Linux is not often pre-installed on laptops. Those wanting to try it generally do so after they have built up some computing experience.

Mac OS X – An operating system used on Apple Macintosh computers.

Microsoft Windows 7 – Microsoft's most recent operating system.

Microsoft Windows Vista – A Microsoft operating system. Vista comes in several versions aimed variously at home and business users.

Microsoft Windows XP – An operating system from Microsoft which has been superseded by Windows Vista but which still remains popular among many users.

MID – Mobile Internet Device. A class of computer recently introduced to provide those who want small-sized computer equipment with an emphasis on Internet or connected communications rather than keyboard-based traditional computing.

Mini laptops – Also known as netbooks. A new class of ultra-small, ultra low-cost laptop.

Mobile broadband – The term used to describe using the Internet over a 3G HSDPA connection. This is done either by having a SIM card slot built into your laptop or by using a small add-on with a SIM card in it that plugs into a USB port on your laptop. All the main UK network operators offer this kind of add-on.

Modem – A device used for mobile communications. Most laptops have a built-in modem which can use the ordinary telephone line for communications. You are more likely to use an external modem for your Internet connection, though. This will be a broadband modem, also known as an ADSL modem.

Netbooks – Also known as mini laptops. A new class of ultra-small, ultra low-cost laptop.

Notebook computer – An alternative term for laptop or portable computer.

Operating system – The main software engine of any computer. The operating system includes facilities that allow software to run and share computer resources, allow hardware to run and allow users to interact with software and hardware via the user interface.

Optical drive – A reader and writer for optical media, typically CD or DVD. Optical drives can be used for a wide range of tasks including playing music CDs, playing commercially available DVDs such as movies, recording onto CD and DVD to make your own music CDs or video DVDs, or to store any files you want to keep.

PAN – Personal Area Network. A PAN is one in which you exchange information directly with another device such as a mobile phone.

Parental control software – If you are in a household with children then you may be concerned about how they could use the Internet. It is possible to restrict their access using parental control software.

PDA – Personal Digital Assistant, the forerunner to modern smartphones. Used to carry diary, contacts lists, documents and other data with you. In their very early days PDAs were unable to be used for mobile communications by voice or for mobile internet access.

Peripheral – A term given to an external piece of hardware you plug into a laptop. There are many examples: keyboards, mice, printers and scanners, for example.

Pixels – The tiny dots that form the image on your computer screen. Computer screens are measured in pixels with the measurements given in height and width.

Plug and play – This term describes hardware that installs all the software it needs automatically when it is plugged into your laptop. You don't need to intervene at all, and the hardware should work perfectly after a short wait.

Portable computer – An alternative term for laptop or notebook computer.

Processor – The 'brain' of your computer. The processor does all the 'thinking', putting information on the screen and working out what you want to do when you click on things, type or otherwise interact with your laptop.

RAM – Random Access Memory. A kind of computer memory. It provides the space a computer needs to store data it is currently using. The most obvious types of data are the applications which are running at any one time, and the information they contain.

Resolution – The number of pixels a computer screen can display. Usually expressed as two numbers – pixels wide by pixels high. For example 1280 × 800.

Rip – The process of transferring media such as music from a standalone medium such as a music CD to your computer where it can be stored and/or moved to a personal media player.

Rugged laptop – A generic term for a laptop with built-in features to help it withstand tough outdoor conditions. Tend to be rather heavier than non-rugged laptops due to the use of strong and solid components.

Scanner – A device you can attach to a computer in order to turn printed material into documents the computer can read. Examples include photographs or important letters you want to store on your computer.

Shareware – A type of software which is usually produced on a try-before-you-buy basis. You can download the software and test it for a period of time before deciding whether you want to buy it or not.

Smartphone – A mobile phone with advanced data management features built in. Can synchronise diary, contacts and other information with your computer, and can be used for web browsing, social networking, document creation, etc.

S/PDIF – Sony/Philips Digital InterFace. A type of connector. Used to connect digital headphones to your laptop.

S-Video – A type of connector. Used to connect a TV to a laptop.

Tablet PC – A generic term for a laptop designed with a touch sensitive display for input via a stylus. Tend to be fairly small and light as they are designed to be used carried in the crook of an arm at least some of the time. Tablet PCs can have stylus or fingertip controls, and can have keyboards or be simple screen only (slate) designs.

Touchpad – An area beneath the keyboard of your laptop which lets you control the on-screen cursor. This is the laptop's most frequently used substitute for a mouse. You move your finger on the touchpad and the cursor moves around the screen to mirror what you do.

Touchscreen – Some laptops have touch sensitive screens. This means you can use either a fingertip or a special stylus to interact with them.

Ultraportable – A term used to describe a certain type of laptop. Ultraportables tend to have a small screen and keyboard. May lack an optical drive.

UMPC – Ultra Mobile PC. A fully fledged computer usually without a keyboard and smaller than any notebook available. Designed for touch screen access. The screens on UMPCs generally don't measure more than 8 inches across the diagonal.

USB – Universal Serial Bus. A connection port that allows you to attach a wide range of peripherals to your laptop, from keyboards to printers and from webcams to modems.

USB flash drive – A kind of portable storage that is mounted on a device which attaches to your computer via USB. USB flash drives come in a wide range of designs and memory sizes vary considerably.

Virus – Malicious software that can cause damage to your data and even render your computer unusable. You should have software to protect against viruses getting onto your laptop.

WAN – Wide Area Network. A WAN operates over a very wide distance, for example a whole country. Large companies set up WAN networks to connect geographically separated offices. The Internet can be described as the world's biggest WAN.

Webcam – A camera you can attach to your computer in order to capture video or still images. Webcams have many uses. Among the most popular is video conferencing over the Internet.

Wi-Fi – The name given to a wireless communications standard widely used for wireless networking. Also known as 802.11.

Troubleshooting guide

Software

Security